# TOO ... TO DIE

## DAVID POTTER

**EVANGELICAL PRESS**

**EVANGELICAL PRESS**
16/18 High Street, Welwyn, Hertfordshire AL6 9EQ England

© Evangelical Press 1982

First published 1982
Second impression 1983

ISBN 085234 169 5

Bible quotations are taken from the New International Version

Cover design by Peter Wagstaff

Typeset in Great Britain by Solo Typesetting, Maidstone, Kent
Printed in the U.S.A.

# Contents

|  | *Page* |
|---|---|
| Introduction | 5 |
| 1. Scene 1: Last act | 7 |
| 2. To die well | 12 |
| 3. All those in favour | 20 |
| 4. Notable distinctions | 31 |
| 5. Those to the contrary | 39 |
| 6. The doctor's dilemma | 73 |
| 7. Help me to live and die | 109 |
| References | 126 |

# Introduction

At a time when the future of thousands of unborn babies was threatened, the voice of Protestant Christian protest was silent. Legislation was passed by the British Parliament in 1967 permitting abortion in certain limited circumstances. We, the public, were told that its main intention was to eradicate 'back-street' abortionists who were alleged to be endangering the lives of large numbers of women. Christians had given little thought to the issues, and some years were to pass before any serious book on the subject appeared in Christian bookshops.

Two things have happened since then. First, the law is now being interpreted so liberally that abortion on demand is almost a fact of life in Britain today. Second, the anti-abortion lobby is now vigorous and many Christians are now active in this movement. However, its attempts to modify or repeal the law on abortion have failed repeatedly.

We may now be seeing history about to repeat itself. This time the issue will be euthanasia. 'Mercy-killing' has become both more common and more acceptable in the last few years. Even Christians are moderating their views to accommodate it. The lobby for legalizing euthanasia is growing rapidly and becoming more and more vocal. It is possible to envisage this happening in the not too distant future. And if once this were to happen then it would be likely to stick. Somehow the drift must be arrested and opinion aroused. So I have written this book to help you form an opinion for yourself.

Now, I must be honest. I have no professional qualifications which give me a 'right' to write. I am not a doctor, nurse or surgeon. I am not a sociologist, psychologist, lawyer or philosopher. I am just a concerned person who used to be a pastor, and who bumped into the subject in the course of working with mentally handicapped people. I was first forced to think about it when asked to speak on the subject, and after two or three years of thinking and reading I felt something ought to be written.

My lack of qualifications does not embarrass me, and I hope it will not embarrass my readers either. We tend to think that 'experts' are the only people to advise on such issues. After all, they are much closer to the problem, which is true — but they can be too close. You see, this issue is not so much medical as moral, and a Christian with his Bible open should be as well equipped as another Christian — be he doctor, lawyer or accountant.

This raises the question of authority. In this book I take the Bible to be God's Word. That has two immediate consequences: first, what it says is accepted as true; and second, it is the highest authority on all matters on which it speaks. God is above and beyond the changing opinions of society and the developing discoveries of science. He has spoken on important issues in terms of higher, eternal principles. At this stage in the book you may not want to accept this basis. As you read on, I hope you will see that the only alternative is 'Every man to his own opinion', which leads directly to 'Every man for himself'.

# 1.
# Scene 1: Last act

Standing at the kerb-side waiting for the traffic to pass, they looked a pathetic couple. Mother must have been seventy-five if she was a day; her son must have been forty or so. She looked tired and frail, while he, loaded with shopping in each hand, looked strong and able. A weekly outing was just over and they were on their way home — they had been to the supermarket for the week's provisions.

The picture has all the marks of ordinariness — unless you happen to notice that he is mentally handicapped. Carrying the bags is no problem to him, but choosing the items needed from the hundreds temptingly displayed is beyond his capability. As for handling money, well, he has little idea what to do. Nor could he care for himself. Living with Mum is not the soft option of a lazy bachelor — he could do no other.

Mother, widowed some years before, struggles under the burden of her increasing frailty, and the strain of caring for her 'boy'. All the while there is a nagging question lurking in the background: 'What will happen to him when I'm gone?' It is a question to which she sees no clear answer.

WARD G4. It seemed to take hours to reach it, down 'miles' of identical corridors painted cream, with highly polished vinyl floors. Ward after ward was passed *en route.* (At least we had only to follow the WAY OUT signs when we left!) The smell of disinfectant was everywhere.

Through the doors of G4 a silent shock awaited us. Rows of white beds, some with cot-sides raised, most of them with a white-faced, white-haired old lady laid against the pillow. Our eyes flickered from one to the other. We smiled as we passed each bed, but the waxen figures did not respond.

Aunty Mary was one of the fortunate ones, sitting out in the Day Room at the sunny end of the ward. She looked as though she had been dropped into her chair rather than seated in it. We greeted her, talked to her, teased her, reminded her — but all the while she sat uncomprehending, unrecognizing, as if we were visitors from another planet.

Sadly we left her. Like all the others in the ward, hers was a meaningless, antiseptic existence. Memory gone, bodily functions uncontrolled, unable even to feed herself, or enjoy her food, she lingered in a hinterland between life and death.

Another ward, another hospital, but here is not the stillness of creeping death. The anguish of delayed death is on the faces of many of its patients. One of them groans weakly, entrapped by drips and tubes. Here many of the beds are occupied by the recently able, by vigorous people now victims of terminal cancer. It is a restless place where drugs, surgery and therapy are combined to ward off the impending approach of death.

And the patient suffers terribly. The suffering of hope in the face of inevitable despair, of surgery which cannot succeed in cure, of therapy which nauseates, of family showing in their eyes their grief at the erosion of their loved one. And as the prospect of success grows more dim, the doctor's vigilance declines with feelings akin to shame at his failure. All the while there is pain, mind-stretching pain.

One more scene, one more hospital, one special ward. Here the atmosphere is different again. It is tense, electric, efficient. This is Intensive Care, a sort of Holy of Holies to the staff. Here medical technology reaches its life-preserving pinnacle — sometimes clutching back from the jaws of death the young lad wrecked in a motor-cycle accident, resuscitating the man suffering from a severe heart attack, and sometimes keeping alive the person who in every other respect seems dead. The T.V. monitor screen by each patient shows by its moving point of light that the patient still holds on to life, the heart still functions. Tubes supply the vital fluids and remove the wastes. And relatives visit to watch helplessly the living death of one they love, fearful lest the point of light should cease to peak, and then the doctors will acknowledge defeat.

These four sad scenes may seem at first to have no connection. They come together with others in a discussion taking place in Britain, and other parts of the Western world. They raise the question whether people should be allowed to live — and die — like that. Ought not every man to die with dignity?

'Nowadays we cannot help thinking about the right to die. The prolongation of life in the Western world in this last half century brings us up sharp against the question, "Life at any price, or can life be continued at too great a price?" Indeed, has the right to live got as its mirror image the right to die?"[1] This is how Dame Eileen Younghusband has posed the problem. As a leading social worker she pointed out that we have difficulty in defining death, which in turn raises questions about our view of life.

'What is the essence of being alive? . . . The dilemma is posed in its most extreme form by great and irremediable mental and physical suffering that cannot be controlled enough to be tolerable. This has always been part of human life but now there are new elements in the situation. People who suffer greatly, or lead a vegetable existence, may now live very much longer and, consequently, at any given time there are more of them, even apart from an increase in sheer numbers.

'This has two aspects: the period of pain and frustrated half-life that many may endure, not part of all the give and take of ordinary human existence; and secondly, the effect of this on those who care for them, whether relatives, friends or professionals.'[2]

No thoughtful human being can be insensitive to these issues. Sooner or later one or other of them will knock at our door, affect our immediate family. We will all have to respond in one way or another, if by that time we still have the freedom to make our own choice.

There is a strong lobby actively at work to try to make euthanasia legal. Like the article quoted above, these people speak of the right to die with dignity, and of the inhumanity of allowing people to suffer. But is this the *right* way to deal with the problems? What solutions are on offer and how do they stand the tests of human-ness and Scripture?

# 2.
# To die well

'Euthanasia' is derived from a Greek word meaning 'the good death'. Its first use in modern times was in 1646: 'A man might be described as making a "good death" when his last days were calm and he slipped into unconsciousness without a struggle.'[3] Others also referred to it during the eighteenth and early nineteenth centuries. Then in February 1873 an article appeared in the *Fortnightly Review* by L. A. Tollemache under the hopeful headline, 'A new cure for incurables'. However, this was not about some elixir of life. We now call it 'euthanasia', for it proposed that the incurable should be given an early death. It was still some time before the word took this use, as in 1887 the President of the Royal College of Physicians wrote a book entitled *Euthanasia*. In it 'he gave detailed advice on how to care for the dying by providing comfort as well as relief from pain and other distressing symptoms. There was no question of cutting life short.'[4]

In the last fifty years, however, this word has acquired another meaning. When the Euthanasia Society of America was formed in 1938, they defined it as 'the termination of life by painless means for the purpose of ending severe physical suffering'. Even that has now been broadened, so that it includes 'death with dignity' administered both to those who request it and those who do not.

The twentieth-century campaign for euthanasia has gradually gained momentum. It is worth noting its progress. A summary of the events looks something like this:

1931. Dr K. Millard, President of the Society of Medical Officers of Health spoke and wrote in favour of euthanasia.

1935. The Voluntary Euthanasia Society formed in Britain.

1936. Bill to legalize voluntary euthanasia presented in the House of Lords. Defeated by 35 votes to 14.

1969. Second bill before the House of Lords defeated by 61 votes to 41.

1976. Incurable Patients' Bill presented in the House of Lords. Strictly speaking this was not a Euthanasia Bill but it did accept the principle of voluntary euthanasia. It was defeated by 85 votes to 23.

1978. Baronness Wooton, sponsor of the 1976 bill, proposed that euthanasia and certain cases of assisted suicide be no longer regarded as criminal offences.

What happens in Parliament is only part of the picture. In the United Nations a Declaration of Human Rights was adopted in 1948 declaring that every human being has the right to life. Strangely, U Thant, the then Secretary General of the U.N., proposed in 1968 that this same declaration should include a statement permitting euthanasia.

'The Euthanasia Educational Fund of New York receives tens of thousands of requests each year for copies of a 'Living Will'. The 'Will' is a short testament addressed to the patient's family, physician, clergyman and lawyer. It says in part, "If there is no reasonable expectation of my recovery from physical or mental disability, I request that I be allowed to die and not to be kept alive by artificial means or heroic measures. I do not fear death so much as I fear the indignity of deterioration, dependence and hopeless pain. I ask that drugs be mercifully administered to me for terminal suffering even if they hasten the moment of death." The Living Will has no legal weight, but the addressees can seldom ignore it with conscience.'[5] Since that was written the Living Will has been enacted as law in several states of America.

Following the defeat of her Incurable Patients' Bill, Baroness Wooton has proposed the use of 'Declarations' in this country. These are essentially the same as the Living Will. The proposal had been put forward in 1969 by Lord Raglan but was defeated in the House of Lords.

In Britain, the Society for the Right to Die with Dignity — EXIT — supplies every member with such a Declaration which, it states, does not ask the doctor to do anything contrary to existing law, but should he be faced with a difficult decision regarding the prolongation of life in the circumstances specified, it would be helpful to him to know the considered opinion of his patient, expressed when in full possession of his or her faculties and when not in great pain or distress.

The Declaration also includes a card to be carried by the person — rather like a kidney donor card, the idea being to tell someone what to do in the event of an accident. It is worth quoting in full:

'Should I be unable to communicate, please note that I have signed, in the presence of two witnesses, the following Declaration:

"If the time comes when I can no longer take part in decisions for my own future, let this Declaration stand as the testament to my wishes:

"If there is no reasonable prospect for my recovery from physical illness or impairment expected to cause me severe distress or to render me incapable of rational existence, I request that I be allowed to die and not be kept alive by artificial means and that I receive whatever quantity of drugs may be required to keep me *free* from pain or distress even if the moment of death is hastened."'

EXIT adds, 'This document is legally binding in so far as it establishes the patient's wishes and, judging from the number of people who sign, it is clearly fulfilling a need. More significant is the fact that it has been welcomed, and in a number of cases acted upon, by doctors.'[6]

Perhaps, then, the law does not need to be changed significantly. A simple 'adjustment' might suffice. In 1976, 'The Criminal Law

Revision Committee in their review of "offences against the person" suggested a new offence of "mercy killing". This would replace the charge of murder in euthanasia cases and make the offender liable to a period of only two years in prison. One of the criteria suggested was that the killing should be with "the consent or without the dissent of the deceased".[7] It was recommended that 'compassion' be accepted as the motivation for this 'offence'.

It would seem inappropriate for the medical profession to join the law-makers in advocating euthanasia. After all, they are committed to the saving of life and the healing of sickness. But from within doctors' surgeries, consulting rooms and medical training schools there is increasing support for euthanasia.

Obviously, the vast majority of doctors spend the greater part of their lives fulfilling the high ideals of their profession. However, they also face the problems raised on the fringes of medical progress. As a result they are often uneasy about black-and-white statements about euthanasia. But the grey areas do not make black-and-white principles irrelevant. They suggest caution in applying them, rather than wilful abandonment of them.

Those doctors and specialists who join the advocates of euthanasia fly in the face of the World Medical Association. In 1950 it recommended to its national bodies that they 'condemn the practice of euthanasia under any circumstance'.[8] Yet a poll of the Association of

Professors of Medicine in America showed that in the early 1970s 87% of those who responded favoured passive euthanasia and 80% practised it. 'At a community hospital [in U.S.A.] researchers found that among staff physicians and . . . students, 59% of the doctors, 69% of first-year students, and 90% of fourth-year students favoured passive euthanasia.'[9] Doctors and nurses find themselves increasingly exposed to subtle propaganda for both active and passive euthanasia.

It is evident that doctors feel themselves under some pressure at this point. The case of Dr Arthur of Derby illustrated this. He was charged with the attempted murder in 1980 of a mongol baby for whom he had prescribed 'nursing care only'. The trial took place at Leicester Crown Court in 1981 — we shall return to it more fully later. His defence was taken up by the Medical Protection Society. They appointed the outstanding advocate Mr George Carman Q.C. as counsel for the defence.

In the course of the trial defence witnesses included the President of the Royal College of Physicians and paediatricians of international repute from as far afield as Aberdeen, Bristol and Barnstaple. Their testimonies showed that the non-treatment of handicapped babies has become widely practised in the medical profession on the principle that there is a distinction between killing and allowing to die. That principle is now established as lawful.

The 'not guilty' verdict was greeted with relief

by the British Medical Association and the British Paediatric Association. Conservative estimates suggested that more than 150 handicapped babies died in 1980 following a decision to withhold treatment — and had the verdict been otherwise, a flood of prosecutions might well have ensued.

According to EXIT, 'Public opinion has for some time been in favour of legal voluntary euthanasia. In 1969 an opinion poll was conducted by Mass Observation Ltd. A representative sample of 2,000 men and women was asked whether voluntary euthanasia should be made possible for people who were incurable and in pain: 51% agreed, 28% disagreed.

'In September 1976, however, the results were much more striking. A National Opinion Poll of 2,121 people found that 69% agreed that "the law should allow adults to receive medical help to an immediate peaceful death if suffering from incurable illness that is intolerable to them, provided they have previously requested such help in writing". Only 17% disagreed.

'Every Christian denomination produced a majority in favour. This included 72% of Anglicans, 71% of Methodists and 77% of members of the Church of Scotland. Even 54% of Roman Catholics were in agreement. This shows that only a small minority of Christians actually oppose the legalization of voluntary euthanasia.'[10]

EXIT does not provide documentation for these astonishing statistics. Nor do they acknowledge that the wording of the poll does not necessarily mean support for legalizing euthanasia.

The media are now turning their attention to the matter from time to time. It seems inevitable that Mr Average will find it a topic of conversation especially when trials of advocates of euthanasia take place. Yet to most people it is such an outrageous idea that they wonder how anyone can possibly urge measures which take life. It is time to look at the arguments put forward in support of this 'solution' to some of life's problems.

# 3.
# All those in favour

The arguments in support of euthanasia fall into three groups, with one further matter which its supporters want considered.

## 1. Please, Sir, may I die now?

It is argued that the right of free choice is a primary moral principle which ought to be incorporated in law wherever possible. State coercion is never right unless the actions of one individual harm others. In this context, 'Since the sufferer's choice to accelerate death does not harm others, it is a permissible exercise of individual liberty and ought not to be subject to the compulsion of law.'[11]

In a nutshell, this is an argument for the 'right to die', which, of course, is not so much a demand that a person be allowed to die — that will happen anyway, sooner or later — but rather that the person should have the right to choose when and how he dies. Although this argument could be widened to take in suicide under almost any circumstances, it is only currently advanced in support of death as a release from suffering and/or senility.

If we argue that every human being has a right to life, then surely the opposite is true — that every human being also has the right to die. Since we have control over our own life why not over our own death also? And if no harm is done to others in the process, why should that right be refused in law? Ought not the state to make the facilities available, to those who wish to use them, for this purpose?

A British doctor, G.J. Goundry, has advocated a 'death pill' for old people who ask for it. In his opinion it will be available and perhaps obligatory by the end of the century. In 1980, Dr Goundry experimented on himself with his 'death pill', with fatal consequences. 'Swedish public-health physician Ragnar Toss wants to open a suicide clinic for the more than two thousand Swedes who will kill themselves each year — "not to treat them but to help them do it".'[12]

In an article entitled 'The Right to Choose Death' (*The New York Times,* 14 February 1972) Professor O. Ruth Russell wrote, 'Surely it is time to ask why thousands of dying, incurable and senile persons are being kept alive — sometimes by massive blood transfusions, intravenous feeding, artificial respiration and other heroic measures — who unmistakably want to die.'[13] If they want to die, and *if* they have no prospect of recovery, and *if* their death will harm no one, do they not have the *right* to die?

## 2. Life is not worth living

Take another look into the geriatric ward. The old lady in the second bed is well into her eighties. Her frail body, her translucent skin, her wispy white hair, all belie the active person she used to be. Seeing her propped against the pillow, with cot-sides raised to prevent her falling out, it is hard to imagine her as a healthy and attractive young woman. She has loved and been loved, raised a family, shared a home, helped others in need, and enjoyed the fresh air on her face. Now she 'sits' in bed unthinking and unfeeling as life drifts past her day after day. Her family comes and goes from her bedside unrecognized and unremembered by her. She sometimes speaks in rambling sentences of the disjointed memories of yesteryear. Her former pride in her appearance has long since gone; now she dribbles slightly all the time, and the odour of incontinence lingers on the air.

Is hers any longer a worthwhile life? By all the normal criteria, probably not. Can she hope to improve and to return to society in due course? The answer is certainly, 'No.' The deterioration of brain cells, the failing functions of the body, the irreversible process of ageing — all point to the fact that she has passed the point of no return. What is the point of her living any longer? Should she not be helped to die peacefully and painlessly?

Or should we ask another question altogether: 'Should she have been allowed to reach this degraded and humiliating condition in the first place?' The writing was on the wall for her some time before. Everyone realized that she was on her last lap. But a few months' rapid decline reduced her to a parody of womanhood. Should she not have been allowed to die with dignity before this appalling vegetable condition was reached? She may be content to linger like this, but those who look on have a sense of horror at what is happening.

This example illustrates the argument that advocates of euthanasia put forward. It is double-edged since it appeals to the right to a worthwhile life or a dignified death. It is appropriate in other instances, too. For example, it applies in the case of persons dying with cancer. They may face the prospect of being hooked up to drips and transfusions, drugged with pain-killers, and suspended part-way between life and death for their last days or weeks or months. There is almost no hope of their ever living a worthwhile life again. As the disease advances they will be left a vestige of their former selves, with their faculties reduced to near zero. They may say, 'Don't let that happen to me. I would rather die!' Or their loved ones may feel that for them. Would it not be more humane, more kind to release them from such a fate before they reach that state?

There is a point beyond which life is not worth living, and when that is reached a person should be helped to die. That is the thrust of the argument. 'No decent citizen would question the obligation to provide services for the severely sick and handicapped that add to their well-being and prevent further deterioration. But part of the dilemma is that sometimes medicine can do this and sometimes it cannot; at some stages of the downward journey it can, at other stages it can only postpone death while the deterioration process goes on to a point where the integrity of the personality is eroded.'[14] Before that situation is reached they should be allowed to die, thus avoiding the embarrassment to them and others of their humiliating decline into a sub-human condition.

'According to Richard Garnett's biography of Jonathan Swift he was so demoralized with, among other tortures, the acute pain in his eye that knives had to be kept out of his reach as were the deadly drugs he craved. "He wanted to commit what the law calls suicide and what vitalist ethics calls sin. Standing by was some good doctor of physick, trembling with sympathy and frustration. Secretly, perhaps, he wanted to commit what the law calls murder."

'For his last three years, Swift sat and drooled, and at least five years before he died in fits of convulsion lasting 36 hours, he had written to his niece: "I am so stupid and confounded that I cannot express the mortification I am under of both body and soul."

'Garnett concludes: "The story of this man's death points us directly to the . . . problem of euthanasia. We get a glimpse of this paradox in our present customary morality that it sometimes condemns us to live, or, to put it another way, destroys our moral being for the sake of just *being*.'"[15]

Dame Eileen Younghusband sets out an alternative: 'Would most of us and those close to us not wish that we may be ourselves when we die? Is it conceivable that some day some people may decide to have some kind of farewell ceremony, or else no farewells at all, when they choose to die? This would mean a big change in our attitudes to death, a change in which close friends and relatives came to say goodbye to someone whose life was over and now hastened the inevitable onset of death. To many of us the idea is abhorrent that anyone should have the right under some circumstances, indeed even social approval, to take into their own hands the time and manner of their death.

'Others may long that this should happen with grace and dignity but not think it should be within their control. The hotly-debated but so far unresolved question is whether for some people, in some circumstances, at some point in time, there should be a right to decide to die whole before their body does so by degrees, the right to decide while they are in full possession of their faculties.'[16]


## 3. Don't be cruel

'The argument in favour of voluntary euthanasia in the terminal stages of painful disease is quite a simple one, and is an application of two values that are widely recognized.

'The first value is the prevention of cruelty. Much as men differ in their ethical assessments, all agree that cruelty is an evil — the only difference residing is what is meant by cruelty. Those who plead for the legalization of euthanasia think that it is cruel to allow a human being to linger for months in the last stages of agony, weakness and decay, and to refuse him his demand for a merciful release.

'There is a second cruelty involved — not perhaps quite so compelling, but still worth consideration: the agony of the relatives in seeing their loved one in his desperate plight. Opponents of euthanasia are apt to take a cynical view of the desires of relatives, and this may sometimes be justified. But it cannot be denied that a wife who has to nurse her husband through the last stages of some terrible disease may herself be so deeply affected by the experience that her health may be ruined, either mentally or physically.'[17] (The second value which the writer goes on to mention is liberty, which we have already considered.)

'In 1624 John Donne, the Dean of St Paul's, wrote an essay in support of euthanasia asking, "Whether it is logical to conscript a young man and subject him to risk of torture and mutilation in war and probable death, and refuse an old man escape from an agonizing end?"

'Even earlier Sir Thomas More, eminent Catholic, wrote in the second book of his *Utopia* that in his imaginary community "When any is taken with a torturing and lingering pain, so that there is no hope either of cure or ease, the priests and magistrates come and exhort them, that, since they are not able to go on with the business of life, are becoming a burden to themselves and all about them, and they have really outlived themselves, they should no longer nourish such a rooted distemper, but choose rather to die since they cannot but live in much misery.'"[18]

Most people not only fear death but also the prospect of dying in terrible pain. Those who advocate euthanasia would urge that genuine compassion would make us agree to release them from their suffering. If there is no prospect of their recovery, and if they will die in a few days, weeks or months, would it not be kinder — some would even say more Christian — to help them to die, thus avoiding an inevitably anguished end? And if it is the free choice of the sick person that this should be done, have we the right to refuse?

The Very Rev. W. R. Matthews, sometime Dean of St Paul's, argued for euthanasia on the grounds of Christian love. 'The great master principle of love, and its child, compassion, should impel us to support measures which would make voluntary euthanasia lawful and which, as stated by the Euthanasia Society, would permit an adult person of sound mind, whose life is ending with much suffering, to choose between an easy death and a hard one, and to obtain medical aid in implementing that choice.'[19]

'Victims of cancer often have to suffer severe

and continuous distress. Pain can be reduced by the repeated use of narcotics and sedative drugs, but often at the cost of nausea, constipation, deterioration of personality, and other distressing side-effects. In addition to pain, victims of cancer may have to suffer the mental misery associated with the presence of a foul fungating growth, obstruction of the bowels, or incontinence, and the utter frustration that makes each day and night a death in life.

'Diseases of the nervous system all too often lead to crippling paralysis or inability to walk, to severe headaches, to blindness and to the misery of incontinence and bedsores. Bronchitis, with its interminable cough and progressive shortness of breath, can have its special terrors which medical treatment can do little to abate in the late stages. Likewise, a patient with a stroke may be conscious but helpless. His misery is frequently overlooked.

'When the alternatives are death with dignity or death accompanied by prolonged pain and distress, common sense as well as compassion support our demand that the choice be the legal and human right of the individual. As the law now stands he has no choice; his wishes count for nothing.'[20]

## 4. Can we afford to keep them?

At the beginning of this chapter one other 'consideration' was mentioned. It is never put to the fore in the writings of the euthanasiasts, but it is almost always mentioned. Nor is it included by them cynically, but seriously and sincerely.

'The fact that we may one day have to face is that medical science is more successful in preserving the body than in preserving the mind. It is not impossible that, in the foreseeable future, medical men will be able to preserve the mindless body until the age, say, of a thousand, while the mind itself will have lasted only a tenth of that time. What will mankind do then? It is hardly possible to imagine that we shall establish huge mausolea where the aged are kept in a kind of living death. Even if it is desired to do this, the cost of the undertaking may make it impossible.'[21] (This paragraph is not a careless aside but part of a deliberate argument made by a leading advocate of euthanasia.)

'One of the under-secretaries of the United States Department of Health, Education and Welfare suggested in 1977 that the various states that did not enact Living Will legislation be penalized by having withdrawn or curtailed the federal funds that would ordinarily supplement state funds allocated for certain major programmes.'[22]

Meanwhile in Britain, 'In one of its papers, *Prevention and Health,* issued in 1976 by the Department of Health and Social Security it was stated, "An increasing number of old people inevitably means more cases of disability and more chronic degenerative disease ... some have questioned the morality of devoting large resources to seeking to extend lives for what must be relatively short periods of time, especially when the quality of such extended life must be open to question."'[23]

In the case of the mentally handicapped the same economic considerations apply. It costs tens of thousands of pounds to provide for the retarded adult after the death of his parents. The capital cost of hostels and homes is vast, and the week-by-week care of them is huge. With almost perpetual economic problems, and with over 60,000 people in need of such provision — over and above the places now available — it is difficult to envisage how this country can afford to meet their need.

The physically handicapped, the chronic mentally ill, the insane and the permanently sick add to the number for whom society must provide. At the same time society must also educate its children, treat its sick, defend its shores against aggression, govern its territory, develop its industry, assist its unemployed — and so on and so on. In a thousand-and-one ways the resources of the country are needed by one and another group, while government struggles both to meet demands and so to tax the people that they do not choose to unseat it at the ballot-box. For the greater good of the greater number should not some, who are a burden to themselves and society — and who can contribute nothing to the general weal — be relieved of their onerous life?

# 4.
# Notable distinctions

Did you feel that one of the four pictures at the beginning of the book was out of place, a sort of 'odd man out'? Three of them were of people who were not about to die naturally. In these cases euthanasia would require some direct and immediate cause to be introduced which was not already present. It might be a pill or an injection, or even some less pleasant means, but it would be *active* euthanasia.

This would not be the case in the fourth picture. The patient on the life-support machine may have been rushed to hospital following an accident or severe heart attack, or may have collapsed under surgery. He is alive by virtue of the swift attention given to him, and thanks to modern medical technology. His condition may steadily improve from 'grave' (strange that doctors use this term about sick people!) to 'comfortable', and after a time he may be well enough to be sent home again. The respirator and the heart monitor may have been required but a short time by the recovering patient. In another case, however, a patient may not have progressed in this way. Severe brain damage, irreversible coma, and dependence on the life-support system may continue and become a more or less permanent prospect. If someone were to switch off the machine this would be described by some as *passive* euthanasia.

The same description would be used in some other cases also. For example, an elderly, senile person might catch pneumonia, thus complicating his already fragile and hospitalized existence. Should prolonged and vigorous efforts be made to keep him alive? Or should he be allowed to slip quietly from life? Passive euthanasia again.

Although 'euthanasia' is used in both instances, the difference between active and passive is immense. One is killing by the introduction of a cause of death which was not present beforehand, even though it may be called 'mercy-killing'. The other permits nature to take its course, so that the patient dies from natural causes.

On this basis 'passive euthanasia' is a contradiction in terms. No measures have been taken to destroy life or to kill — be it mercifully or otherwise. But if the public can once be persuaded to accept that this *is* a form of euthanasia then it is but a step from this to accepting 'active euthanasia'. Our resistance is lowered, even neutralized. One prop in the defences of Mr Average is removed and his agreement is the more probable. It is both more honest and more accurate in this debate to use the term 'euthanasia' only to mean active euthanasia. It is this consent to end life under certain circumstances by active means which is both advocated and sought.

There is another distinction which must be

considered. You will have noticed that in some instances it is suggested that a person will ask to die, perhaps making the request some time before his last illness, or perhaps following its onset. This is called 'voluntary euthanasia'. However, there are other instances where such consent or request will be improbable or impossible. The mentally handicapped or the incurably insane or the senile will not be able, or likely, to ask to die. This is called 'involuntary euthanasia'. We need to look more closely at this distinction.

In the agony of dying a patient asks the doctor kindly to end his suffering with a painless death. In the anticipation of senile decay the elderly person requests the right to die before the process advances. In the frustration of helplessness and dependence the person physically handicapped — by birth or accident — demands to be set free by death. Whether by a Living Will written beforehand, or by his own decision at the time, he is voluntarily requesting euthanasia. To many this is an acceptable proposal. After all, the person is not being 'done to death' against his will. He is simply being helped to do what he himself cannot do — a sort of assisted suicide.

Involuntary euthanasia proposes, less popularly, that for people for whom life is no longer worth living it would be kinder to help them to die rather than to help them continue their empty existence. If the persons in question are incapable of asking to die the decision may be taken for them. It would be the humane way of dealing with the hopelessly defective, the senile, the insane, in short all whose life has degenerated into unthinking existence. The spectre of the state, the medical profession or the lawyers deciding when a person should die is an alarming one.

Dame Eileen Younghusband applies this to the specific case of a mentally handicapped person. 'Even if he is secure and well cared for in his family setting, there is too often the gnawing question: "What will happen to him when I die?" Is the answer years maybe in the backwards of a subnormality hospital or, if there is no better alternative, to be permitted to die peacefully at his parents' wish with his security still around him?'[24]

Already the tide of public opinion is on the turn. In December 1979 Keith Jones was given a two-year conditional discharge after admitting to the manslaughter of his mother. He had watched his father die of cancer, and then his mother became ill with the disease. As she 'lay in pain on her death-bed, he asked: "Do you want me to end it for you?" She whispered: "Yes." Then Jones, with tears running down his face, smothered her with a pillow.'[25] In February 1980 Donald Harding was prosecuted for ending the life of his wife. He was sentenced to three years' probation. Mercy-killing is increasingly acceptable!

'A Dutch housewife may stand trial because she has helped many people to commit suicide. Klazien Sybrandy founded the Dutch Association for Voluntary Euthanasia seven years ago. However, she later left them in order to set up her own Information Centre to give active assistance.

'Since 1976 she has been making appeals to people to hand in certain sleeping tablets, which she passes on to seriously ill people. The public prosecutor has now decided to start collecting evidence against her, though for years she made no secret of her activities. His action follows a complaint against her by a woman in Rotterdam, whose husband ended his life after obtaining advice from Mrs Sybrandy's centre.'[26]

However, there is some uncertainty as to whether this trend will continue or be reversed. This has resulted from the trial of Mark Lyons and Nicholas Reed in October 1981.

Mark Lyons was found guilty on five charges of aiding and abetting, counselling and procuring suicide, and three charges of aiding and abetting suicide. As a member of EXIT he had been sent to help people who had contacted the society asking for its assistance. When he was arrested the police found a suicide kit in his flat containing plastic bags, sleeping pills and elastic bands. They also found notebooks containing his diaries, which showed an obsessive interest in detail, accounts of help given to a number of people and chilling remarks like, 'Took bag 15 minutes to get cold.'

During the course of the trail Lyons appeared as a rather strange person. He claimed to be controlled by a 'puppet master' who had entered his head through a small hole in his skull and had influenced him since childhood. He alleged that this spirit gave instructions by speaking into his left ear! He had also practised as a spiritualist healer and claimed to be a medium.

The methods employed by this seventy-year-old, partially blind man were far from sophisticated. He offered his 'clients' one of two options — all those mentioned in the trial as having died had chosen the first — sleeping pills administered while in bed, taken with alcohol, followed by putting a plastic bag over the head with an elastic band to keep it airtight around the throat; or sleeping pills administered while in the bath, then assisted drowning. And, of course, his travelling expenses had to be paid before the service was performed. By such means he despatched a multiple sclerosis sufferer, a cancer patient, a 'respiratory cripple' and a psychiatric recluse — among others.

The eleven months which Mr Lyons spent in prison on remand, along with a two-year suspended sentence, were considered sufficient punishment for his crimes. The judge expressed the hope that he had learnt a lesson from his experience and that he would no longer pursue his undesirable practices. He seemed to be unaware that while on remand Lyons had offered to help a mentally handicapped man commit suicide while both of them were in the hospital wing of Brixton prison.

Nicholas Reed (aged thirty-three) was a very different figure from his scruffy accomplice. A classics scholar at Oxford, he had risen rapidly in the Voluntary Euthanasia Society, taking over the General Secretaryship in 1978. Within a year he had begun to transform its image. His enthusiasm for the cause led to the publication in 1981 of *A Guide to Self-Deliverance,* intended to help people to commit suicide without 'botching' it. But it was this same enthusiasm which was to prove his undoing. When a team of TV researchers whom he had helped turned over their unscreened film to the Director of Public Prosecutions, this led to criminal proceedings.

Reed was found guilty of conspiring to aid and abet suicide for his part in sending Lyons to those who had telephoned EXIT seeking help. The judge gave him the longest sentence handed out for his crime — two and a half years' imprisonment.

While the trial proceeded there was lively public interest. It undoubtedly accelerated the growth of the Voluntary Euthanasia Society. In 1979 its membership stood at 2,000. By early 1980, due largely to the announcement that it was to publish its book on suicide, it rose to 6,000 members. This continued to increase to 10,000 and during the trial it reached 12,000. And the number continues to grow. The organization has an aura of respectability, having had a peer of the realm as its chairman during 1981, and including among its vice-presidents a physician and a clergyman. Among its supporters it lists professors, broadcasters, a Queen's Counsel, a bishop, a leading Methodist minister and a rabbi. Its executive committee even includes a member of a Community Health Council — a body set up to monitor the activities of health authorities!

The campaign to legalize euthanasia undoubtedly suffered a set-back as a result of the trial. But at the same time another, more subtle fact became apparent, which fits the proverb: 'All publicity is good publicity'. The public reaction had more to do with the methods employed and the people involved than with the results achieved!

The almost involuntary response of most people to euthanasia is to reject it. The idea is initially repugnant. It strikes at the roots of our respect for life. Even when the arguments seem compelling and the mind can raise no reasonable protest, still the heart shouts, 'No.' Is this emotional response the right one? In our advanced society should we accept that the time has come to change the ground rules? What follows is an attempt to begin a reasoned and realistic response.

# 5.
# Those to the contrary

There are problems which must be faced. Only a fool or an ostrich would pretend that the four scenes at the beginning raise no difficulties, or that they are simple to solve. The advocates of euthanasia have faced these problems and looked them in the eye. They have felt them deeply and are trying to provide what they consider to be a compassionate solution.

The Christian also has to look at the problems, and if euthanasia is not the solution, has to provide a better alternative. To do the first and not the second is to fail our Saviour and our society!

Our reply to the arguments for euthanasia may be at two levels. We may offer replies which do not depend on our religious convictions, and we may raise arguments based on the Bible. The first approach will help us say to a non-Christian society like our own, 'There are good reasons for you to withstand euthanasia on the basis of your own non-religious outlook.' We can then go on to strengthen our case by adding arguments which rest on Scripture, and which will appeal to the innate knowledge of God in the unbeliever's conscience. At the same time we will be forming our own Christian view on the subject.

We must make a reasoned and thoughtful response to the challenge with which we are presented.

Too often the initiative in this debate is with those who advocate euthanasia. They press the case with considerable effectiveness, keeping the spotlight on particularly sad cases rather than on basic principles. But, as we have seen, their arguments are sometimes incomplete, at times even far-fetched.

Professor Ruth Russell alleged that there are 'thousands of dying, incurable and senile persons . . . being kept alive — sometimes by massive blood transfusions, intravenous feeding, artificial respiration, and other heroic measures — who unmistakably want to die'. This is simply not true. Such people are not, in practice, 'being kept alive' unnecessarily. Visit any ward for the elderly and you will be hard pressed to find such elaborate equipment and procedures in use. This is a dishonest argument to support a weak case.

Another example of their far-fetched arguments is the incredible picture of 'mausolea' in which the 'living dead' would be preserved for centuries after their minds had ceased to function. Even if it were medically possible, the probability of such ludicrous measures being employed is too bizarre a suggestion to warrant serious discussion.

Let us now turn to matters of principle.

## 1. Some answers with the Bible closed

*a. The right to choose*
The right to die with dignity is proposed as a human right, namely that the person concerned should be free to determine when and how he or she will die. In an age which gives 'free will' and 'freedom' towering importance, it is not surprising that this argument should be given such prominence. But is it valid? Is the person to be killed (mercifully?) free to make the choice?

The argument does not stand close examination, and anyway it is impossible to put it into effect. It leans heavily on the 'right to life' argument and sets over against that the right to die. If we have one, then surely we should have the other. But the comparison falls down, since we are not arguing about the right to *continued* life. The discussion is about *ending* it, and the opposite to that is birth — not living.

Every one of us is alive by some other persons' choice, plus factors beyond even their control! We did not choose to be born, or when or where that event would take place. Nor did our parents control that fact, or make that choice for us. They may have chosen to procreate, but could not precisely determine the conception any more than they could predetermine the sex of the one conceived. In most cases they had little or no choice as to when labour began and delivery took place. So we should at least moderate our boasts about human rights and powers.

We must also recognize that 'no man is an

island' — or to use the Bible's parallel, 'None of us lives to himself alone, and none of us dies to himself alone.'[27] Our quest for independence and autonomy cannot be achieved absolutely. Every life meshes with the life of others. What I do today affects numerous people, from family to shopkeeper, from friend to enemy. The idea that a person could ever take his own life without affecting anyone else is an illusion.

A further question is whether the sufferer is *free* to choose anyway. He may make his choice at one of two possible times: before the onset of suffering or senility, or at the point of suffering. Let us imagine that John Jones decides that he could not face a humiliating or painful end, and writes a Living Will asking to be released by death in the event of either thing happening to him. (We must also assume that the doctor could act upon his will.) Is there any possibility that, when the doctor came to his bedside, syringe in hand, Jones would want to choose a different fate but cannot now express himself? Will his change of mind be regarded as the result of a clearer view of life and death, or will it be put down to his being 'befuddled by illness'? The permitted executioner cannot be sure that the wish expressed two years previously is the choice of today.

The sufferer may choose to die when overwhelmed by his painful or pathetic condition. This voluntary decision is supposed to be made 'only if the victim is both sane and crazed by pain'.[28] This poses a problem which an American lawyer expressed thus: 'By hypothesis, voluntary euthanasia is not to be resorted to until narcotics have long since been administered and the patient has developed a tolerance to them. *When,* then, does the patient make the choice? While heavily drugged? Or is narcotic relief to be withdrawn for the time of decision? But if heavy dosage no longer deadens pain, indeed, no longer makes pain bearable, how overwhelming is it when whatever relief narcotics offer is taken away too?'[29]

A British doctor poses the same question, writing about euthanasia by prior consent: 'Either the candidate volunteers in view of *future* distress, or he volunteers in a mind disturbed by present distress. How can a man decide the degree of distress he is likely to tolerate at some future date? Who is to measure it when it occurs? When he is distressed, and then signs the form, can his judgement be regarded as natural?'[30]

'The supporters of voluntary euthanasia lay heavy stress on the right of the individual to choose death as an alternative to "suffering from a painful and incurable physical disease". This definition is imprecise and it is important to consider the practical consequences of voluntary euthanasia as, strangely, this does not seem to have been done. The interpretation as to what this means is left to the subject, relatives and doctors to determine. When does a stroke, diabetes, heart disease, rheumatoid arthritis or chronic bronchitis and emphysema, which are all common, incurable and occasionally distressing diseases qualify for the giving of euthanasia? How is "suffering" to be precisely defined? What is "painful" and how is the degree of pain that is complained of measured and quantified? Physical diseases commonly have emotional overlay, depression and despair magnify many symptoms. How are these excluded?'[31]

After a course of pain-killing drugs a patient is frequently hypersensitive to pain. The mental side-effects are said to outlast the pain-killing effects by many hours. 'A person in terminal stages of cancer who had been given morphine steadily for a matter of weeks would certainly be dependent upon it physically and would probably be addicted to it and react with the addict's response.'[32]

Not only may the drugs affect a person's power to choose rationally; but the emotional see-saw set in motion by pain will also influence the power of free choice. One man who has been on both sides of the problem is Dr Benjamin Miller, an American. He wrote from personal experience: 'Anyone who has been severely ill knows how distorted his judgement becomes during the worst moments of the illness. Pain and the toxic effect of disease, or the violent reaction to surgical procedures may change our capacity for rational and courageous thought.'[33]

The same point was made by Lord Horder, speaking in one of the House of Lords debates: 'During the morning depression he (the patient) will be found to favour the application under this Bill, later in the day he will think quite differently, or will have forgotten all about it. The mental clarity with which the noble Lords who present this Bill are able to think and speak must not be thought to have any counterpart in the alternating moods and confused judgements of the sick man.'[34]

Unlike voluntary admission to a mental hospital, the decision that one's life should end allows no second chance. Once the choice has been made and put into effect the patient is irreversibly dead! The argument for free choice is encrusted with barnacles large enough to sink the proposal. But there is still another consideration.

What of the members of the family involved? Where is their freedom to choose when it comes to this predicament? It may become an emotional tug of war for them, or it may be the looked-for opportunity of entering into their inheritance! On the one hand they will want to resist all steps to shorten the life of the loved one, and at the same time long to see him or her relieved of suffering. On the other hand they may look with hopeful anticipation to the pecuniary benefits awaiting them.

No husband would want to see his loved wife suffer agonies in the last days of life. He would urge doctors and nurses to take all means to relieve her pain. On the other hand he would not want their time together to be foreshortened by irrevocable death ahead of time. Imagine the emotional burden of having to approve a request to die under such circumstances — and the shame and guilt of remembering that decision for the rest of his life.

There are other families where such love is cynically remembered. The patient has become an unwanted encumbrance. If his last illness is in the family home, then all the anguish and inconvenience of that adds further weight to the burden. Resentment grows with impatience at the lingering life of the sick relative. In response to such an atmosphere, or as a direct result of pressure brought to bear upon him, the patient may 'choose' to die. It is hardly a free choice — and the physician may suspect that this is so. Must he do as requested?

Nor is it unknown for an elderly and infirm person to be urged — and offered help — to die by relatives looking forward to their bequest. A case which came before the British courts in 1979 involved a nurse who tried to persuade her mother to accept help to die, so that the daughter might resolve her own tangled financial affairs.

'No one should blind himself to the fact that what we are seeing is not an issue of a voluntary kind at all. It is a battle between ideologies which condition men's minds and so partly govern their "voluntary" decisions. The modern assertion is that atheistic "freedom" should supplant religious conditioning. What nonsense: atheistic Humanism is itself a religion, with a basis of faith and a system of beliefs.'[35]

## b. The possibility of a mistake

An old person will grow older — and will probably become increasingly frail and dependent on others. A mentally handicapped person will continue to be mentally handicapped, and therefore never able to live a fully independent life. But the future of persons suffering from a seemingly incurable illness is less certain. Yet it is for such as these that the advocates of euthanasia make their strongest plea that they should be free to choose to die.

For all their professional skills, doctors sometimes make mistakes. 'To err is human'! But a wrong diagnosis will probably mean that the patient does not respond to the treatment prescribed; in which case the doctor will review his lack of progress, and reassess his own original analysis of the illness. If he wishes, he may try a different course of treatment which may be more or less successful. But consider another possibility. Suppose the doctor has wrongly diagnosed an illness as incurable, and suppose further that the treatment which would normally be given would be either painful or very unpleasant, and suppose that, after discussion with the patient, euthanasia was resorted to rather than the hopeless discomfort of unavailing treatment. Despite all the truth of what was said about the disease from which the doctor *thought* the person was suffering and its treatment if, after all, he was not suffering from that disease, there would be no second chance after the final injection!

The advocates of euthanasia are aware of this

difficulty. One of them put it this way: 'Doctors are only human beings, with a few if any supermen among them. They make honest mistakes, like other men, because of the limitations of the human mind.'[36] This is a risk we accept when we go to see our general practitioner. But if doctors have the power of death as well as life, we must ensure that there are *no* mistakes.

Dr Benjamin Miller was left to die the death of a hopeless tuberculosis victim. His illness dragged out over five years, with sixteen periods in hospital. It was then discovered that he was suffering from a rare malady which affects the lungs in much the same way as T.B. He told the story of a brilliant doctor, Richard Cabot, renowned for his ability to diagnose illness. On the occasion of this doctor's retirement, 'He was given the case records (complete medical histories and results of careful examinations) of two patients and asked to diagnose their illnesses ... The patients had died and only the hospital pathologist knew the exact diagnosis beyond doubt, for he had seen the descriptions of the postmortem findings. Dr Cabot, usually very accurate in his diagnosis, that day missed both.

'The chief pathologist who had selected the cases was a wise person. He had purposely chosen two of the most deceptive to remind the medical students and young physicians that at the end of a long and rich experience, one of the greatest diagnosticians of our time was still not infallible.'[37]

Another mistake the doctor may make is that

of assuming that there is no hope of a cure being discovered in the lifetime of the patient. He adds the role of prophet to that of doctor. It may be that there is no cure at the present, and that the likelihood of a cure being available in time is not great. But once the lethal dose has been given the patient will be dead — and whatever unexpected developments there may be will be of no help to him. They have not yet found a cure for death either!

Such errors of judgement are, thankfully, relatively few — at least, one assumes that they are since there is no way of demonstrating this one way or the other. But the fact that they can happen, and occasionally do happen, should give us pause for thought — especially if there is a possibility that euthanasia would increase the number of those who *die* from wrongly diagnosed disorders.

'Everyone has an irremediable disease as soon as he is born, which shows obvious physical signs at some time between the ages of 40 and 60. The real thrust of prognostic uncertainty (i.e. predicting the course of the illness) is not merely that some may die by mistake. It is that everyone, at least if over 40, is in principle a candidate for euthanasia if these ideas are followed to their logical end.'[38]

*c. The wedge*
Now for the argument the euthanasia lobby likes least of all. It runs something like this: if we allow people to be killed for any reason, includ-

ing painful illness, senility, insanity etc., it would be the thin end of the wedge, leading to all sorts of horrors in due course. To which the reply is given: 'Not so! Any proposals would be carefully monitored, and the procedures carefully controlled to prevent abuse.' Which is right?

We have to look at the way things have gone in the past. Experience shows that there is a real tendency for any lowering of standards to lead to their being lowered still further.

In the 1970s abortion became a fact of life (or death!) in Britain. The House of Commons had passed David Steel's Bill, and assurances were given that its contents were very limited. The circumstances under which abortion could be obtained were few, and clearly defined. The safeguards were more than adequate to protect the unborn baby. In less than a decade attempts were made to tighten the law because the reality of the situation was more akin to 'abortion on demand' than the intended compassionate and limited use of abortion. Once the pro-abortion lobby had the wedge in position, it was relentlessly hammered home.

What happened in Germany during World War II was not an imaginary horror story. In the 1930s and 1940s the same tendency was evident. It began even earlier when the idea that there is a 'life not worthy to be lived' was popularized. Once that was accepted in the minds of the nation, other things were bound to follow. Nazism is notorious for the atrocities committed against the Jews in the concentration camps and the gas chambers. But Jews were not the only ones to be discarded. German veterans of the First World War, one-time national heroes, were liquidated if they had lost limbs as a result of their heroic struggle for the fatherland! Elderly, retarded and handicapped people were 'released from their suffering'. With sham compassion they were driven to their deaths in buses supplied by The Charitable Transport Company for the Sick.

This is not to suggest that every advocate of euthanasia has a Swastika tattooed on his heart! Indeed most of them are angered by comparisons with wartime Germany. They also loathe that brutal regime and are motivated by a deeper compassion. But what we have to point out by reference to the pogroms of the 1940s is not a comment on these people. It is a comment on human nature in general.

Even within the euthanasia movement the same trend to broaden the base for helping people is apparent. When the Voluntary Euthanasia Society was founded in 1935, it campaigned for legislation permitting help for the incurably ill to die. They now also call themselves 'The Right to Die with Dignity Society' or EXIT for short. Both their name and their literature imply a more liberal approach. They have in fact taken things a step further by setting up a working group to consider campaigning for non-voluntary euthanasia. So as not to lose support and credibility for EXIT, they are looking at the possibility of establishing a separate organization to promote this cause.

Scaremongering is not our business. Proponents rightly object when their proposals are caricatured as a 'Watch out, Granny, you are eighty next week' campaign. They do not advocate the right of the state to 'put down' its elderly. They do not propose that the handicapped should be hounded out and put to death at a certain age. But if they will not acknowledge that the most careful legislation will be broadened, that the initial acceptance of euthanasia will lead to less acceptable proposals, then they show no sense of history, and little insight into human nature. Indeed they ignore the evidence of recent history in their own ranks. The two members of EXIT found guilty of aiding and abetting suicide did so in respect of elderly and seriously ill people. But they were also found guilty of conspiring to aid and abet in the case of a twenty-four-year-old man with a drink problem who was depressed. He changed his mind before it was too late. There would be no way to halt this broadening of the categories if once euthanasia was permitted by law, even in the most restrictive terms.

### d. These also ran

Taken together, the above objections are very substantial arguments against euthanasia. But they are not all that can be said. Other considerations also merit some mention. They are not so much arguments against euthanasia as issues which bear thinking about, if there is to be any legislation to allow euthanasia of any sort.

What effect would the introduction of euthanasia have on doctor-patient relationships? At the moment it is normal for there to be genuine trust between the two sides. The patient knows that the doctor will make every effort to find and remove the cause of illness, pain, depression, and so on. But even though this is the case, some people are afraid to visit their doctor for fear that he may find that their ache or pain is incurable, or even a symptom of a fatal disease. How much more they might fear a visit to his surgery if he also held the power to end the patient's life! At present it is comforting to know that in the event of terminal illness the doctor will usually do all he can to ease the last days of a dying man. There is no threat, no fear, when the doctor rings the doorbell or walks into the ward. But were he to have the power of death, imagine the terror of wondering whether the next injection might be fatal!

What effect would legalized euthanasia have on medical research programmes in due course? These are hard enough to finance at the moment, but there is good reason for the country to afford them. If euthanasia is introduced it destroys the incentive, and hard economics would second the motion that such projects be abandoned — unless they benefit those who will live anyway. How will discovered cures be tested? Who will want to use them? It will change the attitude to medicine. Let an illustration help us here.

Back in the 1960s a Conservative government

introduced legislation to liberalize divorce laws to a small extent. It was argued that this would help to sort out the tangles in which some marriage relationships were enmeshed. But no one asked what this would do to the whole concept of marriage in our society. In the ensuing years not only has divorce become easier to obtain, marriage has become less significant. A parallel can be drawn with euthanasia. It will not only become easier to allow people to be killed, but it will also make the saving of life less important.

Another concern, felt more particularly by the medical profession, is who will administer euthanasia. Doctors who have written on the subject say that it will divide the profession into those who would and those who would not. Some suggest that a second profession should be set up to deal with it — a sort of medical executioner! Then suppose that the patient/sufferer decides that his life should now be terminated. By his 'free choice' he places an intolerable burden on another person, one which the practitioner would not be able to refuse if legislation had given him the necessary power. Strange freedom if it results in such liberties!

Whether or not such a division was made, it would certainly affect the attitude of doctors. The medical profession was largely opposed to abortion prior to 1967. When the law changed, however, doctors became legal abortionists on a wide scale. They were then compelled to defend their position. If Parliament attempts to reverse the abortion laws doctors would have to oppose such moves. They have blood on their hands!

The same would inevitably happen with regard to euthanasia. At the moment the medical profession is largely opposed to its introduction. If they found themselves having to carry it out under law, they would have to rationalize their position — or admit to being murderers of defenceless, dependent people. The damage to their professional and personal integrity would be incalculable. As seen in the trial of Dr Arthur referred to earlier, eminent professors and consultants may be called upon to defend a man who does as they do — even if the action is questionable. The judge warned one witness for the defence of the danger of incriminating himself by his testimony. But those who have allowed handicapped babies to die must defend the practice for the sake of their own consciences.

There are two other considerations which lie on the border between a Christian and non-Christian outlook. They originate with the gospel and its attitude to people, but are not now exclusive to those who profess to believe in the Bible. They are 'the sanctity of life' and 'compassion for the needy'. However, since they do find such strong support from the Bible, we shall deal with them in the next section, along with other arguments which that inspired book gives us.

The present section can best be concluded with a quotation from the flyleaf of Dr Everett Koop's book on abortion and euthanasia. It is taken from the writing of a French biologist,

Jean Rostan. 'For my part I believe that there is no life so degraded, so debased, deteriorated or impoverished that it does not deserve respect and is not worth defending with zeal and conviction . . . Above all I believe that a terrible precedent would be established if we agreed that a life could be allowed to end because it is not worth preserving, since the notion of biological worthiness even if carefully circumscribed at first, would soon become broader and less precise. After eliminating what was no longer human, the next step would be to eliminate what was not sufficiently human, and finally nothing would be spared except what fitted a certain ideal concept of humanity.

'I have the weakness to believe that it is an honour for a society to desire the expensive luxury of sustaining life for its useless, incompetent, and incurably ill members. I would almost measure a society's degree of civilization by the amount of effort and vigilance it imposes on itself out of pure respect for life. It is noble to struggle unrelentingly to save someone's life as if he were dear to us when objectively he has no value and is not even loved by anyone.'[39]

## 2. Some answers with the Bible open

Does a Christian have the right to impose his 'religious' views about euthanasia on a non-religious society? If his views are right; he not only may do so; he must make his reasons known to others, regardless of their attitude to religion. It is his moral duty. We have already seen that there are sufficient objections to the proposed 'death programme' to make it repugnant and unacceptable to us as human beings. And since Christians are members of our society they have the right and duty to share in forming its views.

Nor should we be embarrassed at putting forward arguments based on the Bible. In the first place, we are sharing the truth, and truth is truth whether or not a person is prepared to accept it as such. He may want to imagine that he lives now, say, in 1932, and however much he objects to being told that this is not so, his objections do not alter the truth of the matter. Similarly, what God has revealed in the Bible is a *true* description of the human condition. It is God's Word, written under His inspiration and from the perspective of absolute, comprehensive and universal knowledge. Consequently it is invariably accurate, it agrees with observable reality, it is unerringly reliable and inevitably relevant to the life we must live both individually and corporately. But more than this, it has divine authority. While we should not use the Bible like bigots, we need not apologize for using its arguments on any subject on which it speaks.

In the second place, we must not forget that the non-Christian is also equipped with a conscience given and 'programmed' by God. He has an innate knowledge of right, as it differs from wrong. Admittedly that conscience is sadly mutilated following man's rejection of God in the person of our forefather, Adam. But there is ground on which we may stand; we have something to which to speak and we may do so with authority. We already have an advantage.

Someone may point out that the word 'euthanasia' is not found in the Bible. And this you may expect, since we regard this as a modern issue. However, this is not the reason for its receiving no mention. Both suicide and assisted suicide were known and practised in Greek and Roman society. Yet the Lord Jesus never once referred to either as an option for sufferers. In their letters the apostles answered many contemporary problems and warned of the inevitability of suffering. Yet they never mentioned euthanasia as an escape route.

It has been suggested that King Saul approved of euthanasia when he asked his servant to kill him. It is highly doubtful whether that is a reasonable interpretation of his request. He was more concerned that both he and the nation should not suffer the humiliation of the king being captured by the enemy. The writer of 1 Samuel certainly does not express any approval for his request. His subsequent suicide is part of the tragic story of a man who departed from faith in God and whose death was in measure a judgement on his life.

Although we may not find direct reference to this subject in the Bible, that is not to say that it fails to help us at this point. It sets out principles governing life and death, living and dying, which help us to evaluate the persuasive arguments in favour of euthanasia. Let us now turn to some of those principles.

*a. God is in charge*
This is the first argument in order and priority. In more traditional theological terms it says, 'God is sovereign.' The Bible makes it plain that God is in control of everything. He is Lord of the universe, King of all rulers, Supreme Power of all powers, whether they are heavenly, earthly or hellish. The Bible opens with the words: 'In the beginning God . . .' It closes by assuring us that God is on the throne of heaven. And, in between, everything else it says is consistent with this view of God. The description is not simply an idea, or an ideal. It is a matter of fact!

This truth has staggering implications. It means that there is nothing which happens in the world of which God is not aware even before it takes place. What He has not directly caused, He has allowed to happen. This must be seen to be true in respect of every individual — in his millions! When this is recognized we realize that God has immense power, knowledge and wisdom.

Admittedly, this presents us (not God) with some problem. We argue about the origin of evil, about human responsibility and free will. We try to avoid fatalism on the one hand, without falling into the pit of anarchy on the other. But as we read the Bible, we find that not only does it show us a God who is in control of literally everything, but also that man is both responsible and accountable for his own actions.

He must answer to God for what he does. If our minds are so limited and our logic so restricted that we cannot reconcile these two concepts, we have to admit that both appear in God's order of things, and that the Bible consistently teaches that this is the way things are.

If we can travel far enough to accept this, we can go further still. God, as sovereign Lord, controls also the issues of life and death. Job saw this: 'In his hand is the life of every creature, and the breath of all mankind.'[40] The psalmist saw it too: 'My times are in your hands.'[41] The apostle Paul saw this: 'In him we live and move and have our being.'[42] Every writer of Scripture regarded it as simply a matter of fact. And, apart from cases of suicide and homicide, life today confirms this view of man's dependence on God in life and death. Man does not have the power to create life, nor can he prevent the taking of life by God in heart attacks, illness and old age.

It is not surprising, therefore, to discover that there is a divine order in the lives of human beings. In the poetry of Ecclesiastes it is expressed like this: 'There is a time to be born and a time to die.'[43] And, on reflection, we have often seen how timely a person's death proved to be – even if, at the time, it seemed untimely!

Now we must relate this principle to the issue in hand. Do we have, or dare we take, the right to decide the time and direct cause of a person's death? The answer must be, 'No!' Even if, from our perspective, his life seems meaningless and without hope, we must still say, 'No.' We cannot guess what a day of life holds for that person and how it will affect him, or us, or others. Again, the writer of Ecclesiastes put it cogently: 'Since no man knows the future, who can tell him what is to come? No man has power over his spirit to retain it; so no one has power over the day of his death.'[44] To take to ourselves the sovereign right to kill, on the basis of our small view of the issues, is to act both stupidly and unkindly. We would be behaving like a man who, from his perch on a step-ladder, imagines that he is better able to assess the size of a crowd than is a police officer in a helicopter!

It is God's prerogative to decide the time of birth and death. If we accept that He is both just and kind, wise and loving, then we can be sure that these qualities will influence the way He deals with people. And since He sees from the perspective of time and eternity, we may be sure that He takes into account every consideration that bears upon the matter.

Such a truth requires Christian humility and trust: humility to acknowledge God as God, and trust to accept that He does everything well. We shall return to this theme again shortly.

*b. Man and his life*

Whether Christian or not, most people believe in the sanctity of life. No thoughtful person regards living things as disposable like paper handkerchiefs! And human life is especially regarded as important and worth protecting. Scenes of war and brutality on T.V. news bring a sense of disgust and horror to people of every class and colour. The waifs and strays in the wake of war, earthquake and famine evoke a multi-million pound reponse from nation after nation. What lies behind this generosity? Why not let the dying die, the hungry starve, the homeless freeze? Because life is too valuable, even sacred.

This is a surprising response from a society which is generally committed to the view that life is just a series of coincidences, the climax of a mechanical process of evolution, where the survival of the fittest has been the main 'moral' influence. But if the non-Christian with such an outlook feels that life must be preserved, how much more should the Christian feel like this! He sees man as the product of special creation, where human beings have been particularly marked out from the animal kingdom. Man bears the likeness of God! This amazing fact we learn from the Bible. That 'image' has been broken by sin, but just as the broken shards of a gorgeous but smashed vase all bear its pattern and decoration, so every facet of disjointed humanity points to its wonderful original. We reason and talk, we listen and play, we enjoy and dislike, we are fulfilled or hungry — we are different from everything else in the world.

This is why the crime of murder is especially detestable in God's sight. Its evil lies not merely in that another creature has been destroyed, as if men and insects were all on a level. It is because man is made in God's image. That is why God regards the death penalty as the proper punishment: 'Whoever sheds the blood of man, by man shall his blood be shed; for in the image of God has God made man.'[45] When God gave the Ten Commandments it was to be expected that He would include 'You shall do no murder.'[46]

Human life is especially sacred, whether or not a person is handicapped. It has God's mark and stamp on it — a mark denoting both origin and ownership. What pip-squeak of a human being (be he the most eminent medical professor or consultant) dares to lay a finger on it or presumes to determine when it should be snuffed out? Breathtaking audacity!

This concept that man is wonderful because made like God also gives human beings their dignity. As we have seen, the advocates of euthanasia use 'dignity' as an argument for ending life. But dignity does not consist in dying with your hair brushed, your false teeth in place, your glasses on and perhaps your mind alert. It is something different from that. Dignity is not merely a matter of decorum, for you can find among the tramps of London's embankment those who, from their breeding or education, still hold themselves upright among the scruffs. It is something which distinguishes us from the animal world, in that we are not chased off to die in a hole, or alienated from the pack when we grow weak.

To die with our dignity intact does not require that we are hustled out of life at the convenience of others, or by some well-meaning physician embarrassed at his failure to find a cure. Nor is it to be sedated with sleeping pills and then to have a plastic bag pulled over one's head — as was done by a member of the Right to Die with Dignity Society in the practice of euthanasia. It is to die in due time surrounded by those who care about us as a person, who tend our needs compassionately and enrich our closing days with a feeling of worthwhileness even to the very end.

'It is vital that we put first, *not* economics or efficiency charts and plans but being *people* — real flesh and blood people. We are not to be materialistic robots who think and act like machines and will even kill to maintain their lifestyles. This attitude is as stupid as it is wrong. It is stupid because such people have traded their beautiful humanity for sawdust and ashes — for broken homes, for abortions, for starved children, and for old people locked away and even destroyed. Being a person has infinitely greater rewards for those who will consciously concentrate on being people — warm and loving people — rather than on personal peace and affluence.'[47]

### c. Purpose and suffering

If God is in charge to the extent that He controls life and death, it is not surprising to discover that His control extends to what happens between the two. The Bible shows that God actually has a purpose for each life.

It is comforting to know this. What has happened to me today was part of His plan for me. I had no heavy sense of destiny weighing me down. One thing seemed to lead to another. Much of it was very ordinary. But when I step back and see what has happened in the past week, or month, or year, or decade — then a pattern emerges. Although I may not have realized it at the time, I was part of a plan. A purpose was prepared in heaven and worked out on earth. God did the planning. I prayed for it to happen: 'Thy will be done, on earth as it is in heaven.' And that is what happened.

There is no shortage of Bible texts to illustrate this. God explained it to Jeremiah when the young prophet was first called into God's service. 'Before I formed you in the womb I knew you, before you were born I set you apart; I appointed you as a prophet to the nations.'[48] God persuaded Ananias to go to the newly converted Saul of Tarsus by sharing with him a glimpse of His plan for the future. 'Go! This man is my chosen instrument to carry my name before the Gentiles and their kings and before the people of Israel.'[49] All the Old Testament promises of a coming Messiah presuppose this divine control — even to the fact and the time of His death by crucifixion. 'This man was handed over to you by God's set purpose and foreknowledge . . .'[50]

Because God acts with purpose life can be hopeful for the Christian. We are certain that God's goodness will accomplish good. More than this, even death can be hopeful, too. As the door of death opens before us and closes behind us, in that instant the Christian is ushered out of a sorrowful, sinful world into the immediate presence of the Lord Jesus Christ.

All of this stands in stark contrast with the euthanasia proposals. Its advocates must say, necessarily, that there is no hope. Theirs is a counsel of despair. They look at the life of the dying man and say, 'There is no purpose in keeping him alive.' Of the retarded adult they say, 'This life is meaningless.' Of the senile elderly they ask, 'What's the point?' The only positive thing they offer is the ultimate negative — the end of life.

We must now go one step further, because this does highlight another problem — the problem of suffering. If God is in charge, why does He not do something to stop the suffering in the world? After all, if we human beings want to stop it, surely He must want to as well. The difference between us is that He can and we cannot!

It is a matter of plain fact that God both allows and orders circumstances which result in suffering — sometimes in judgement, sometimes in love, sometimes to improve, sometimes to test, sometimes to correct, sometimes for personal good, sometimes for the good of others involved, sometimes to strengthen faith, sometimes to weaken pride, sometimes to teach and always, *always* with purpose! We may not understand or see that purpose at the time — or ever — but we can be assured that life is purposeful.

The problem of suffering is much wider than can be tackled in this short book. But since it cannot be ignored either, let two quotations from larger books give a summary of the Christian view on this subject.

First of all from Herbert Carson's excellent book *Facing Suffering*: 'The Christian is persuaded that this world is not [a] blind alley. The present physical universe is not the extraordinary outcome of some fortuitous convergence of material forces. History is not some turbulent stream of events tumbling over the rocks and finally losing itself in the sands of meaninglessness. The world bears the stamp firmly laid on it of a purposeful Creator. History bears clear evidence, not of the interplay of blind economic forces or of mere material factors, but of the providential direction of a personal God.

'The world about us bears the mark of the curse of God, but it also gives clear evidence of the grace of God. History exhibits all the cruelties and vices of sinful men, but it is also vibrant with the redemptive purposes of God. So pain is not some accidental excrescence on life to which one can only react with a shrug of despairing acquiescence. Even in pain there is meaning to be found, and the Christian aims, not merely to survive the buffetings which suffering brings, but to learn the lessons which God is teaching him. His faith is not a prescription for survival, but is the divinely-given key to unlock some at least of the mysteries of the pains and griefs which inevitably beset him.

'To put this in personal terms and at an individual level, the Christian faces his own suffering with challenging questions. He does not ask merely, "How can I find strength to face this test?" This question he certainly does ask, and the answer he discovers in the grace of God. But it is not the final question. The ultimate query is "What is God teaching me through this time of suffering?" Allied to that is the further practical consideration, "How am I to apply the lessons I learn to my own profit, to help others, and above all to glorify God?"'[51]

The second quotation is from John Wenham's, *The Goodness of God*. 'No Christian dare doubt God's goodness in permitting the most grievous suffering, when he remembers the means God chose for the overthrow of evil. It was in the depth of human agony that Christ "bore our sins in his body on the tree". Not only tortured in body and forsaken by his friends, but cut off from his Father and become "a curse for us", he suffered what no other man has suffered. But in dying he won the decisive battle against human sin and against the cosmic hosts of wickedness which have enslaved the world. On the cross "he disarmed the principalities and powers and made a public example of them, triumphing over them". What an amazing thing that God should choose this little planet as the scene of the final conflict with evil! What a reassuring thing that he should have chosen suffering as the means to the accomplishing of his ends. What a source of strength to know that he does not ask of us more than he was prepared to give himself . . . There is much that the Christian cannot understand, but in the darkest hour he can trust.'[52]

Now let us relate this to the main issue under

consideration. When a baby is born with a permanent irreversible handicap which will result in long-term problems, it is not an accident from God's point of view. There is a purpose in it. If we end the life of that person — whether sooner or later — we fight against, even destroy, that purpose in part or in full.

When a middle-aged man is stricken with a terrible disease and wastes away before the eyes of his loved ones who look on helplessly, it is not a tragedy upsetting God's plans. Euthanasia would seem to frustrate the purpose behind the suffering.

For the old person bewildered by living there may be no apparent reason to allow him to stagger to his end. But he is not alive by man's choice. Nor should he die by man's choice, else the intention of God is unfulfilled.

We may bear God's image, but we do not have His authority. We may share His wisdom, but only to a very limited extent. We cannot take it upon ourselves to act as if we were God Himself! But what about those who suffer? Are we to be indifferent to their sufferings? By no means! But we will come to that later.

*d. Real compassion*
One of the strongest weapons in the armoury of those who advocate euthanasia is their appeal to compassion. Any discussion on the subject tends to be in terms of heart-rending examples, leading to the suggestion: 'Wouldn't it be kinder to end it for them?' We cannot ignore the challenge of

this. They reprove their opponents for not caring sufficiently about the suffering of others, and tell them that they are cruel to be so indifferent. Surely, they say, love will dictate that we set people free from their pain, humiliation and despair.

It sounds well, but if we think more deeply for a moment some ugly questions will arise in our minds. What sort of compassion is it that says to a man, 'There is no hope for you. Die now'? The last spark of his humanity is trampled under foot as if he were no more than an insect. What sort of love is it that despises the life of an old person who is content to drift unthinking from day to day? A person in pain may prefer to die if he cannot live free from his agony. But is that the only option love can offer? Will no one extend a hand of friendship so that even painful life will be better than painless death? And if someone can find a remedy for the problem of pain why should it not be made available to all in his position?

If you were searching for *real* compassion, would you look for it in someone who took life, or in someone who preserved and even gave life? Jesus Christ is history's plainest example of what love is. It is evident from the accounts of His life that He cared about people. He urged His followers and His critics to love those in need — and He showed them how to do it. He was untiring in His efforts on behalf of the outcast, the sick, the blind, the poor, the hungry, the paralysed, the hopeless and the bereaved. Although

His contemporaries in Greece and Rome practised abortion and euthanasia, He had no part in it, nor ever suggested that this was the course for true compassion.

But it was not only as an example and teacher that Jesus lived. He made the ultimate sacrifice — He willingly surrendered His own life for others. Since suffering — mental, physical and spiritual — is a direct result of sin, He dealt with the problem at source, and in the only way possible — by dying in the place of sinners. Being without any sin, He alone could do this, and in doing so He bore an infinity of suffering. And all because He loved!

In fact the whole gospel is a declaration that God is love. Holiness requires justice, and God is holy. Love meets its demands. And God is love, not just because of what He does — it is the way He is! His love has its source in eternity past, flows through the present, and on into eternity future. So when people suffer or linger, when tragedy strikes, when hearts are near to breaking under the pressure of great burdens, God *cares*. The Man who died for us rose from the dead for us, ascended for us. There is now a Man in heaven who has felt what we feel, who can sympathize with our weakness.

If we claim to believe in Him, and to be motivated by His Spirit in our lives, then we should show the same compassion. We have to face the problems squarely and *do* something about them. We cannot say to the advocates of euthanasia, 'There is no problem.' We cannot allow the pain-racked simply to suffer, the vacant merely to exist, the retarded to be dumped. If we will not let them die at the hand of another, we must do something for them while they live. But before we consider what we should do, there is one more aspect to be considered.

# 6.
# The doctor's dilemma

By now, some of my readers must be thinking, 'That's all very well, but what happens if . . .?', which is a common reaction. In fact, the discussion of euthanasia usually turns on what to do in particular cases, rather than on matters of principle. No matter whether it is a debate among professionals or two people sitting on a bus, this is commonly the case. It is natural, and perhaps inevitable, that our thoughts turn to the difficult examples with which suffering confronts us. We must not dodge the issue. Whatever our theoretical conclusions, they must be worked out in practice. But we must proceed *from* principles *to* practice, or else we shall drive through the problem in reverse gear.

We do not find perplexing those areas of the subject which are black-and-white. Everyone can see what to do when the issues are clear-cut. It is the indefinite shades of grey which cause us difficulty. To highlight this, let us imagine for a moment that euthanasia has become an established fact of life and is used to regulate our society. As a result of this progress any handicapped baby is not allowed to survive the diagnosis of its problem. An equal number of boy and girl babies is ensured, with a view to fair distribution later on. Any excess of males or females are disposed of at birth. At the other end of the age range seventy-five years is considered an adequate life-span and a gentle death is arranged for all who reach that age. Between the two extremes society assists the demise of anyone ill for more than sixty days.

What a nightmare world! None of us would agree to that. The issues are so plain. Such proposals would not begin to find acceptance with any right-minded person. Nor, as far as I know, would advocates of euthanasia propose such a scenario. The issues appear to be black and white.

But in the real-life debate which is taking place today there are large grey areas. In almost every radio or television discussion on euthanasia the argument is in terms of particular cases. Every doctor knows and faces the problem. In the course of his working day he finds himself asking very hard questions: 'Should I continue to treat this person, or should I let him die?' He may ask the family for their view and they then must share his dilemma. Indeed, the family may create the dilemma for him by asking that he withhold treatment from their new-born handicapped baby, or their increasingly senile parent. We, too, must face such problems.

We must first acknowledge that doctors are only human beings. They have no sovereign right to determine issues of life and death. Their knowledge is necessarily limited. Their ability also is restricted. We have all heard complaints against them when it has taken some time for them to diagnose an illness, yet it is common knowledge that one set of symptoms might well indicate several different disorders in a patient. The task of the medical profession is to try to sort out which is which. We must not expect a divine insight into our problems by those who, like us, are mere men and women.

Doctors must also recognize this limitation. They are in danger of assuming, wrongly, that theirs is the right to determine life and death in their patients. There is both room and need for a measure of humility in the face of great responsibility. No one, be he pastor or archbishop, general practitioner or consultant, is above an obligation to determine actions in terms of principles.

It might seem impertinent for me — a non-medical, non-professional person — to presume to tell the 'experts' what (or what not) to do. To side-step that accusation I intend to let the professionals speak for themselves. These lengthy quotations may help to show that the practical problems can, and must, be dealt with so as to honour what we are as people. They must be dealt with in terms of the principles we have already worked out.


## 1. Opposite dangers

The long process of training a doctor moulds his

outlook so that he can keep two great enemies in view. One enemy is immediate — illness; the other is ultimate — death. He must by all means conquer the first. The sick must have their ailments accurately diagnosed. A proper course of treatment must be prescribed, as appropriate. The longer-term health and welfare of the patient must be ensured. By the time he has qualified, this will be the doctor's reflex response to illness. It will drive him on when he is perplexed or dispirited, and will produce a concern for his patient at the expense of concern for himself. The spectres of disease and death must be exorcized by his own skilful use of the tools, techniques and therapies with which his professional education and experience equip him.

However, the doctor is not a miracle man or a god. There are, inevitably, times when illness will not let go its hold and death steals closer to the patient day by day. Understandably the doctor reacts to this — and may do so in two opposite ways.

*a. Embarrassed disinterest*
Failure is humiliating to us all, and especially for a doctor who sees it as costing the life of his patient. It may be an embarrassment to discover that he is not able to do all he promised. The patient's hollow eyes seem to reprove him for his failure. The medical charts mock his ability. It is easier now to pay less attention, to evade the relatives' questions about progress.

'In recent years, medicine has become so

orientated towards prevention and cure that the dying patient is regarded as a failure. He is moved to a remote corner of the ward, or to a sideroom, and visits by the medical staff become infrequent and cursory. Nurses tend to avoid the patient except when duties demand or the call-bell is rung. An atmosphere of despair develops, a combination of a feeling of helplessness — "there's nothing more we can do", and a sense of hopelessness as death challenges the shallowness of society's death-denying philosophy of life . . . death is seen as the ultimate disaster, the obliteration of a once vibrant personality, and terminal care as a kind of macabre play.'[53]

I had an interesting conversation in a train while writing this book. I was working on the first draft of the manuscript and had some of the books I had researched on the table as well. An elderly lady, who had been sitting across the gangway, slipped into the seat beside me. 'Excuse me, but do you mind if I talk with you,' she asked. I put my pen down ready to listen to her. She had been a widow for about a year and having noticed the books I was reading wanted to tell me what had happened. Her husband had become unwell, and was eventually found to have cancer. Surgery proved helpful, but not for long. Soon he was ill again and drugs seemed not to bring any improvement. He became progressively weaker until it was obvious that the end was not far off. In spite of his considerable pain, the doctor called less and less often.

One Friday the doctor told her that her

husband would not last the weekend, but he himself would not be on duty to visit in an emergency. On the Saturday the husband became very ill, and suffered acute pain. His wife phoned the surgery for help. None was immediately forthcoming. She had to sit with her husband through a terrible night. On Sunday morning the doctor who called seemed less than concerned and gave only a little relief to the suffering man, and even less to the burdened wife. His visit was as brief as decency would allow. Again the nighttime brought awful anguish to the old couple, until at last the husband slipped out of life and his wife slept, exhausted, by his cold body. She told the story without bitterness. Her faith in God had brought her through that, but she felt great sadness at the way her dear husband had been left to die so painfully. I asked whether she would have preferred the doctor to administer euthanasia before such suffering became inevitable. She squared her shoulders and spoke with strong but quiet emphasis, 'No.'

It would be wrong to give the impression that such was in any way a common example of the attitude of general practitioners, but it would be equally wrong to pretend it does not, or cannot, happen.

*b. Meddlesome medicine*
'There is little doubt that doctors and nurses often add to a patient's suffering by giving inappropriate treatment. Stomach tubes, drip-feeds, antibiotics, respirators, cardiac

resuscitation are all supportive measures for use in acute or sub-acute illnesses to assist a patient through a critical period towards recovery of health. Normally to use such measures in the terminally ill, with no expectancy of a return to health, is bad medicine. A doctor has a duty to sustain life: he has no duty — legal, moral or ethical — to prolong the distress of a dying patient.

'"Meddlesome medicine" is not always wholly the fault of the medical personnel involved. Sometimes doctors are actively encouraged to prescribe inappropriate treatment by relatives unwilling to face the inevitable.'[54]

Sandol Stoddard writes in crusading style in support of hospices. Her tendency to overstate her case must be acknowledged but at the same time her point must be taken.

'We have needed a dictionary to help us recover the ancient connection between the objective thing, hospital, and the embracing act, hospitality. It is a strange embrace, the one we now find welcoming us to the place called hospital. It is one that neutralizes instantly whatever life force it is that makes each one of us into a unique individual. Hospital welcomes my body as so many pounds of meat, filled with potentially interesting mechanical parts and neuro-chemical combinations. Hospital strips me of all personal privacy, of all sensual pleasure, of every joy the soul finds delight in; and at the same time, seizes me in the intimacy of a total embrace. Hospital makes war, not love.

'Our young medical soldiers in the media are so brave, so attractive, one wants them always to win. There is a mystique about this war against death that makes us turn our heads away on those who are hopelessly, incurably ill; and also from those who are quite consciously ready to die. These are the ones that disturb our picture of the way things ought to be. From "hospes" to "hospital" the psychology has changed from one of love to one of war, and in the psychology of war, force is imperative. Therefore we arrive at the strange, new embrace that pins the inert body of a man or woman, terminally ill to a machine that forces that person's body to breathe without even knowing its name.

'It is our attitude toward death, I believe, that has so badly skewed and spoiled our contemporary sense of how persons who are well ought to relate to persons who are sick.

'"Death is un-American," Arnold Toynbee remarked . . . The death of a patient is perceived as a humiliation and an outrage by the average physician in our culture; to the nursing staff in an acute-care hospital, it feels like a personal defeat . . . For indeed, why should such an untoward thing such as death be allowed to happen in our society? The very look of a modern hospital identifies it as a fortress, an armoury, a place of battle. The doctors dressed for combat with their engines and their weapons of cold steel — are they not the Knights Errant of our modern Crusades? If death succeeds in storming such walls as these, who has been at fault? Who has slept on watch? Or, has there been a traitor within?'[55]

Literature advocating euthanasia abounds with stories of people whose lives are not unlike those Sandol Stoddard describes — but the conclusions drawn differ from hers. Professor Norman Anderson summarizes such accounts like this: '[The] stories describe how patients are sometimes subjected to painful surgery, or distressing medication, which only serve to prolong, for a very limited period, a life which is not really worth living, instead of being allowed to die in peace; of elderly persons whose arrested hearts are reactivated by massage in circumstances which do little more than give them the doubtful privilege of "dying twice"; of those who can never recover consciousness but whose biological life is maintained by some artificial means; and of people so distraught that they deliberately attempt suicide only to be forcibly resuscitated and thereby driven to make the same attempt again in even more distressing circumstances. Cases like this, it is said, may provide outstanding examples of the way in which doctors fulfil their duty to preserve and maintain life, but fall very far short of fulfilling their complementary duty of compassionate care for the suffering.'[56]

Even the most ardent supporter of life versus euthanasia would hesitate to condone such practices. It is not living for the sake of breathing which Christians must advocate — as if passing oxygen through the lungs constituted life. Our modern problem has been complicated by the amazing and wonderful advances in medical technology. These save many a person from death and are used primarily for good. But there are those for whom they may make continued breathing possible, but not a real or viable life. In other words, it is now possible for a doctor to keep a person 'alive' by extraordinary measures when it is questionable as to whether what he is doing is right.

## 2. A time to stand back

Do you recall the dying of President Tito of Yugoslavia in 1980? News of his ebbing life was broadcast daily until repetition became monotonous and the story dropped from the newscasts. Weeks passed before the final announcement of his death was made. There may have been political considerations for keeping the eighty-eight-year-old ruler 'alive' for so long. Frantic efforts were also made to keep former President Eisenhower from death.

One quotation could well both open and close discussion. A professor (Norman Anderson) quotes another professor (G.R. Dunstan).

'As Dunstan insists, "The notion of patients continuing endlessly wired up to machines is fictitious", for such machines are — or certainly should be — employed only "as temporary aids, either while remedial attempts are made, or until it is discovered whether the organism, unsupported, is capable of spontaneous function or not.

When hope of recovery is gone, the machine is switched off, the artificial support is removed." The most difficult problem is provided by the comatose or decerebrate person, whose "spontaneous vital functions continue, because the lower centres of the brain which control them are the only part of it unharmed; the cerebral cortex, which enables rational self-consciousness, is destroyed". In France and Sweden, it seems, this situation is regarded as actually constituting death, but of such a person Dunstan confidently asserts: "He is not 'kept alive'; he lives, and while he lives, he is entitled to elementary human care, that is nursing care, simply to be fed, turned, kept clean. Whether an attack of pneumonia, say, should be countered with active therapy, like an antibiotic, is another question; appropriate management might rather be to let the body fight its own battle, win or lose — there is no obligation, in such a case to administer a particular remedy." And then he asks, "Who are the others said to be 'officiously kept alive'? They are the old, the senile, the mentally handicapped of every age." — and he rightly asserts that "All they claim from us, and about all they are given, is the basic human claim, to shelter, warmth, food, elementary medical and nursing care, and a little companionship".'[57]

That seems to me a most reasonable position to take. Death is not determined in terms of breathing, but in terms of brain-death, the irreparable breakdown of the central nervous system. What I am trying to say is simply this: there is a time when the doctor can and should stand back. Let a doctor tell how he sees this for himself.

'Let me illustrate. There is a unique tumour of childhood called the neuroblastoma in which I have been interested for more than thirty years. Because of this I have developed a broad clinical experience with the behaviour of this tumour as it affects the lives of my patients and I have perhaps had more neuroblastoma patients referred to me than would normally be the case, because of my special interest in this tumour. I present this background in order to establish the fact that with this particular tumour I have considerable expertise in understanding the clinical course and have been able to predict with relative accuracy what will happen in a given patient when certain signs and symptoms occur or when certain responses to treatment are known. In a given situation I might have as a patient a five-year-old child whose tumour was diagnosed a year ago and who, in spite of all known treatment, has progressed to a place where although her primary tumour has been removed she now has recurrence of the tumour (metastases) in her bones. On the basis of everything I know by seeing scores of patients like her I know that her days of life are limited and that the longer she lives the more likely she is to have considerable pain. She might also become both blind and deaf, because those are sequelae that might be expected when this tumour spreads in the bones of the skull.

'If this five-year-old youngster is quite anaemic,

her ability to understand what is happening to her might be clouded. If her normal haemoglobin should be 12 and it is now 6, I have two choices. I can let her exist with a deficient haemoglobin level knowing that it may shorten her life but also knowing that it will be beneficial in the sense that she will not be alert enough to understand all that is happening around her. On the other hand I could be a medical purist and give her blood transfusions until her haemoglobin level was up to acceptable standards. In the process of so doing she would become more alert, she would be more conscious of the things happening around her, she would feel her pain more deeply, and she might live longer to increase the problems presented by all of these things.

'In the second place there are anti-cancer drugs which I know beyond any shadow of doubt will not cure this child, but which may shrink the recurring tumour in several parts of her body, postponing the inevitable death by a matter of a few days or weeks. However, it is possible that the effect of these drugs will not be very dramatic on the tumours in the skull. They may relentlessly expand, producing blindness and deafness. Would it be better to let this little girl slip into death quietly, with relatively little pain, and with her parents knowing that she can both see and hear — or should we prolong her life by two or three weeks, increase the duration and intensity of the pain she would have, and possibly run the risk of the added terrible complications for the family to witness: blindness and/or deafness?

In such a circumstance I opt to withhold supportive measures that would prolong miserable life for the patient to bear and the family to see.'[58]

Someone may swoop on this touching story and shout, 'Passive euthanasia.' Not so; that is to over-simplify the issue to a ridiculous extent.

'It is widely recognized in the medical profession today, for example, that a surgeon contemplating a palliative operation on an elderly patient should ask himself the question: "Would this procedure give him a *reasonable* chance of an *appreciable* duration of *desirable* life at an *acceptable* cost of suffering?"; for although none of these adjectives can be exactly defined, all of them should be taken into consideration in the course of making a responsible medical decision. In so far as this is possible, moreover, the whole position should be explained to the patient, who always has the right, when conscious, to refuse to submit to surgery. Similarly, when the life of a patient suffering from terminal cancer is threatened by an attack of pneumonia, for example, it is wrong to describe as "euthanasia" a doctor's responsible decision that his duty of care is best fulfilled by withholding antibiotics — or, in other circumstances, that the time has come to cease to grapple with the fatal disease and to concentrate exclusively on its symptoms, and thus to allow the patient's life to draw to a peaceful close. And precisely the same principle applies to the administration of whatever drugs, in whatever quantities, may be necessary to relieve severe pain. In many cases these drugs may, of course, have the side-effect of marginally shortening the patient's span of life, although sometimes the relief of pain and anxiety have precisely the opposite effect; but there is, in any case, an essential difference between a determination to relieve suffering in order to minimize the trauma of death and a deliberate decision to precipitate death in order to end the trauma of suffering.

'Now it is, of course, perfectly possible to argue that it is exceedingly difficult to make any valid ethical distinction between causing a person's death by some positive act, on the one hand, and allowing him to die by some deliberate refusal or failure to act, on the other. But this argument is, I believe, wholly out of place in the present context where allusions to what is sometimes called "passive" or "indirect" euthanasia are most misleading. The dilemma with which the doctor has to grapple is not an abstract problem in the field of ethical theory but the practical question of what is the proper treatment for an individual patient in particular circumstances. And here a number of different factors are involved. He has a clear duty, for example, to preserve his patient's life in any acceptable way, but this does not imply a duty to prolong the process of dying by what may aptly be termed "meddlesome medicine". Again, he has a complementary duty to relieve his suffering by any legitimate means, but these do not include the deliberate prescription of a lethal dose.'[59]

## 3. Should a handicapped baby live?

There is yet one more situation to which we must turn by way of applying the principles set out so far. What is to be done with a handicapped baby? Should it be allowed to die at birth, or should it be helped to live? This has become an emotionally charged issue in recent years, especially with regard to those born with spina bifida or Down's syndrome (mongolism). It affects these two types particularly because their handicaps are immediately recognizable at birth.

Every couple hopes that their baby will be healthy, with all his or her physical and mental faculties. Most have their hopes fulfilled, but one in every 100 live births is mentally handicapped, and a smaller proportion are physically handicapped. Though comparatively few are thus born subnormal or abnormal each one represents a sad disappointment at least, or at worst a crushing blow to the parents.

Those whose handicap is obvious and considered sufficiently serious at birth can be dealt with in a way which can spare the family and the child much suffering, and at the same time relieve society of a long-term burden. The baby can be allowed to die — a simple case of passive, involuntary euthanasia. Is this right, legally and morally? Apparently it falls within what the law allows, but the question of its morality still waits an answer.

It is now time to look more closely at the trial of Dr Leonard Arthur and its consequences.

Dr Arthur is a consultant paediatrician at Derby City Hospital. He is a man of high reputation. On the day after the verdict the editorial in *The Times* stated, 'Counsel for the prosecution, defence counsel, judge and jury (by implication of their verdict) alike paid tribute to the high professional standing, conscientiousness, humanity and true motivation of the accused . . . A paragon charged with the heinous crime of murder.'[60] The *Sunday Times* referred to him as a 'holy doctor', noting that he had a New Testament with him in the dock, that his father was a vicar, that one sister and a daughter are married to missionaries, and another sister and daughter are married to vicars. In his statement after the trial Dr Arthur thanked people for their prayers.

As *The Times* pointed out, 'The explanation of the paradox is that while the proceedings had the form of a murder trial they were really a test-case in medical ethics. The question at issue was not that of guilt or innocence in any ordinary sense but that of the duty of a doctor who was in charge of a new-born baby of severe and irreversible deformity whose parents wish him dead.'[61]

At 8 a.m. on 28 June 1980 baby John was born suffering from Down's syndrome. Having examined the child, Dr Arthur discussed the matter with the parents who told him that they did not want the baby. The case notes were then marked, 'Parents do not wish the baby to survive. Nursing care only.' He also prescribed a drug known as DF118 to be administered every four hours in liquid form — the only 'nourishment' the child received. By 2.15 p.m. that same day it had already begun to take effect. It was not until 1st July, after hours of gasping for breath, suffering muscle spasms, and now with a distended stomach, that the baby finally died. The toxic level of the drug in the baby's body was three times a fatal level for an adult. The case for the prosecution was that Dr Arthur caused the death of the baby — a charge of murder. During the course of the trial the charge was changed to attempted murder when evidence was presented showing that the baby was suffering from other deformities which may have contributed to its death. However, it was alleged, Dr Arthur had intended the baby to die.

For our purpose there is one particular facet of the trial to be noted. It was the united front presented by members of the medical profession. A brilliant case was made for the defence by Mr George Carman Q.C. He called one medical witness after another to show that an important distinction is made between killing and allowing to die. Where a baby is grossly malformed at birth it may be given nursing care only, with such medical help as will free it from discomfort in dying. This will usually take place only if the parents have given their assent. And it appears that this is in line with the ethical handbook of the British Medical Association, which implicitly admits that, should the parents so wish, a doctor may decide not to treat a severely malformed infant. In the event this was endorsed by the jury in declaring Dr Arthur not guilty of attempted murder.

So much for the trial itself. What of the issues it has raised? It did not prove conclusive in those matters which are so vital. Should a handicapped baby be allowed to die? How handicapped should it be before this is agreed to? Who should decide? There are no simplistic answers. During the trial Sir Douglas Black, president of the Royal College of Physicians, stated that in every case there are three variables: first, the clinical situation of the child, which may range from normal to very extreme handicap; second the parents' attitude, which may range from loving acceptance to revulsion; and third, medical management, which may range from no intervention to advanced surgery. Since no two cases present the same combination of those variables the doctor must act in terms of principles. And that is just what we have been trying to set out in the course of this book. These are appropriate whether the 'patient' is a handicapped adult or a terminally ill adult. We must now apply those principles in trying to suggest a response to the particular problem posed by the birth of a handicapped baby.

We have already declared that God is sovereign in every area of life, and human experience. The paediatrician standing by the side of the newly born malformed baby should recall what God said to Moses when he complained of his lack of eloquence: 'Who gave man his mouth? Who makes him deaf or dumb? Who gives him sight or makes him blind? Is it not I, the Lord?'[62] Nor should that be taken to suggest that God is a vicious deity taking malicious delight in distorting helpless lives. Far from it. The Bible shows that He is particularly concerned for the welfare of the weak and handicapped. 'Those who take advantage of their disabilities will be an especial target of divine wrath (Leviticus 19:14, Deuteronomy 27:18). To propose that the handicapped should be singled out for death goes against the whole spirit of biblical law, which insists that the godly have a special duty to protect the weak members of society, those most easily exploited by the unscrupulous.'[63]

Furthermore, 'the Old Testament looks forward to the messianic age as one in which God will open the eyes of the blind, and "the lame man shall leap like an hart, and the tongue of the dumb sing for joy" (Isaiah 35:5-6). And of course the Gospels often allude to such prophecies in interpreting our Lord's healing ministry (e.g. Matthew 11:5).'[64]

The direct consequence of declaring that God is sovereign is that He has a purpose in His ordering of human affairs. That does not cease to be the case simply because a handicapped baby has been born into a family. I saw my life's work as being that of a pastor, and the fact that my first child was born with Down's syndrome did not seem to have any bearing on that prospect. Indeed it was not until she was ten years old that there seemed any possibility of change. But her presence in our family had developed an awareness of a need faced by those who have retarded children – the need for some long-term care when the families can no longer cope. That awareness has since been shaped into a charity providing that sort of care, and has become the whole-time expression of my own Christian service. While this may be more dramatic and obvious than in many cases, the principle holds true in *every* case that God has acted with purpose in entrusting a handicapped life to a family.

This in turn leads on to another aspect of the problem. We dare not give parents a right which God gives to no human being – that of disposing of human life. To quote the editorial in *The Times* yet again, 'Parents' wishes in these tragic circumstances deserve every respect, but they must be set against the proposition that their child is not wholly at their disposal: every live-born baby enters civil society and by doing so acquires independent rights, of which the chief concerns life itself. He is no less entitled than the rest of us to receive all available life support.'[65]

To allow parents to decide that their child should die in one particular case will lead inevitably to wider freedom to do so. Indeed Mr Carman Q.C. argued thus in the heat of his defence of Dr Arthur. 'When a baby is born, who are the people who care most and are most involved? It is the mother, the father and the doctor. If they make a decision together in consultation that the baby be allowed to die because that was the decision made in this case, it will be my submission to you that that is a decision that the law permits and humanity recognizes.'[66] That is a sweeping statement suggesting far more than merely dealing with a handicapped baby.

In the end, however, some guidelines are required to give expression to principles in real-life situations. We might wish that the issues were black and white, that every handicapped baby should be kept alive in prospect of its living a happy and worthwhile life. That is not the way things are! Some babies are born grossly malformed and appallingly handicapped. Their hold on life is fragile and their prospects slight. Should they receive such surgery as they may require to live? What if they become ill — should they receive treatment? How much should be done to keep them alive? This is the grey area, where absolutes are harder to discover and apply.

Some say that the issue we have to consider is the quality of life the baby may be expected to enjoy. Momentarily that may seem both useful and helpful. But how can we know what this will be? The doctor may describe its present condition, but he cannot take the role of the prophet and predict its future development with any certainty. Indeed most parents of Down's syndrome children have found that the medical profession has shown a distinct weakness in this predictive role. Perhaps it is because it only sees the most severely retarded returning again and again for consultation and help that it assumes that all such children are doomed to a worthless life. Parents often have been faced with a negative outlook from the doctor. On a BBC TV *Panorama* programme in November 1981 one mother told how she was visited by the paediatrician the day she gave birth to a mongol baby. He told her that the child would be severely retarded, would never walk or talk, would be doubly incontinent, and might also be blind and deaf — did she want to keep it? 'Yes, I do!' was the emphatic reply. And in the event not one of the predictions was fulfilled. Such parents have often been told to 'put the child away and forget you ever had it'.

Even if doctors were able to predict with certainty the prospects a baby had for its future development, 'quality of life' would not prove a helpful criterion for deciding whether it should live or die. After all it is a very subjective standard. What might be an acceptable quality of life to one person might be unacceptable to another. Malcom Muggeridge wrote scathingly on this point in *The Sunday Times:* 'It requires no great prophetic power to foresee that the trial and acquittal of Dr Arthur may likewise be expected to prepare the way for acceptance of euthanasia as part of our contemporary way of life. At first, it will be a matter of disposing of seriously handicapped children who, for whatever reason, may be plausibly regarded as unlikely to appreciate the full quality of life available today — that is to say, to travel, drive a motor car, have sex, watch television, and otherwise relish the devices and desires on offer in the twentieth century.'[67] On that basis most of the Third World population would also be candidates for discreet disposal!

Indeed if 'quality of life' is admitted as a satisfactory basis for deciding on the life or death of handicapped babies it could not be long before it is applied to others. Yes, the wedge again — or the slippery slope!

While we cannot argue for an easy solution to this issue, there is one other possibility which may help us to apply right principles to difficult situations. We may discuss the possibility of deciding on the grounds of 'viability'. That must not be taken to infer, in this context, financial considerations! Far from it. Rather it is to suggest that we ask whether the handicapped baby can be expected to survive without permanent *intensive,* high technology, medical care. It is possible that a child may be born with a lethal handicap, so that, even though it is nurtured and nourished, it cannot live for long. (It is at least reasonable that it be offered that much chance to survive!) It is simply not going to prove to be viable. Therefore, while maintaining essential support and care, one recognizes that an early death is probable, and every measure is taken to make it as comfortable as possible.

Another child may be born with a handicap that is serious in that it is inevitably permanent, but need not prove fatal. Immediate surgery may be required to relieve some secondary problem, and this should be carried out if, apart from that, it may be expected to live without permanent intensive care. The case of baby Alexandra demonstrated the application of this approach. She was born in August 1981 with Down's syndrome and with the additional complication of an intestinal blockage. Her parents refused to consent to surgery and asked that she be allowed to die. She was made a ward of court and the operation was carried out successfully. She lives healthily and happily with a foster family.

Of course, every handicapped child will require a good deal of extra help and support throughout its life, but that is no reason for its not being allowed to live. Where there is the prospect of life it should be given every help to do so. When the doctor sees that intervention is required then he may apply the standard already quoted: 'Would this procedure give him a *reasonable* chance of an *appreciable* duration of *desirable* life at an *acceptable* cost of suffering?'[68]

## 4. These lived, to die well

Here are three examples of people who would today be regarded as 'suitable cases for euthanasia'. Yet each account shows how unsuitable such a course of action would have been. They lived to use their lives well. They are but three of hundreds, even thousands, of similar instances, some of which are even more dramatic. In these examples the positive approach to life and death was born out of a real and personal faith in the Lord Jesus Christ.

Many times during his life Martyn was seriously ill, even at the brink of death. On the basis that his deformed body would never allow him to live normally, and would make him totally dependent upon other people all his days, it might have seemed prudent to allow him to die as early as possible. Had euthanasia been legalized his parents might often have been urged to consent to it. In fact, Martyn lived for almost twenty-seven years, a life which had a profound impact on many people. At his funeral, some 300 people gathered to pay tribute to his memory. And the university where he was studying for a Doctorate of Philosophy established a memorial prize. Let his father tell more of the story.

'I cannot remember a thicker November fog. My wife sat in the back of the car as I drove in the heavy South London traffic. She was oblivious of the problems all around us and showed no anxiety at all. Her mind was too full of happiness and gratitude to God, for we were bringing our son home from the maternity hospital. The Lord had given him to us after five years of waiting and we felt that he was a precious gift indeed. Could we have known the future would our contentment have been less? Would it have been better, as some folk today are saying of such cases, if he had not been suffered to live? Martyn was unable ever to set his foot on the ground and walk, never to know normal life with all its varied possibilities, never even to turn over in bed or raise his arms above his shoulders. All this was mercifully hidden from us that happy November morning. Would it really have been better if he had been "put down"? Looking back on his twenty-seven years of life and all that he achieved in spite of his severe handicap there can be only one answer, an emphatic "No". He brought us much sorrow and anxiety but, in God's wonderful enabling, he brought us tremendous joy and wonderful enrichment. A handicapped life need not be an unhappy life nor need it be futile.

'At first we had no thought that anything was amiss. He seemed a perfectly normal child, if anything, more contented and more placid than most infants. He would never kick off the coverlet or struggle to sit up when he had been laid down to rest. This was so slight a matter that we scarcely recognized it to be unusual. But, as the months passed, when other children crawled and pulled themselves up on their feet, he made no such effort. When we tried to encourage this and set him on the ground his legs would not support him. At first the local doctor and then, later, the specialist we consulted, told us it was only slow development. But the day came when we learned that he had been born without the normal muscles. He would never be able to do the things other children did. He would spend his life in bed or in a chair. He would have to be washed, dressed and fed by others and be taken everywhere he went, completely dependent upon us and particularly on his mother. He was liable to be frequently unwell with chest infection. His mother was not to know an unbroken night as long as he lived and his life-expectation was very short. Was this too heavy a burden for her to carry? Would it really have been better if he had not survived birth?

'Today we just thank God for every day that we had with him, and we rejoice to know that many beside ourselves thank God for him. In the Lord's goodness Martyn was physically handicapped, but otherwise he was perfectly normal. His brain had suffered no damage. His body was imperfect and as the years passed became terribly twisted and bent, but he was granted the full use of all his faculties apart from this. What is temporal in our creation was incomplete, but what is eternal, mind and spirit, was unimpaired. He was obviously bright, happy and intelligent. He early learned to talk and developed a singularly wide vocabulary for his age. He became a great reader. His rather frequent bouts of chest infection were very patiently borne. He had resilience. The London Education Authorities provided him with home tuition and then, later, a place in a school for handicapped children. Then he went to boarding school in company with other physically handicapped youngsters. It must be acknowledged that he found absence from us hard to endure. Inevitably the home centred round him rather much. He was splendid company, rapidly gaining a remarkable general knowledge that was widely based.

'When Martyn was eight he came to know the Saviour for himself. Though young, he had a definite experience and made a sincere committal of his life to Him. From then on he never looked back but made steady spiritual growth. The church to which he was regularly taken had an evangelical and Bible-teaching ministry. His home was often visited by Christian friends, ministers and missionaries. He developed spiritual maturity beyond his years. He was a natural academic and in due time entered university. All through this time it was his mother who made it possible for him to attend school and college, taking him and bringing him home daily. His great interest was history and theology, reading very widely in both. He enjoyed the university atmosphere, making many friends, and whenever possible filling our house with them. He graduated with a first-class degree and in the opinion of the department, had he lived, would have made a worthwhile contribution to historical scholarship. Most important of all was the influence of his character. In the Christian Union and in the local church his life truly counted for God.

'Martyn's life was short and severely restricted but his achievements were real. Physical handicap and bodily weakness do not limit what God is able to do in a life that is committed to Him. This indeed he proved, and all who knew him testify to it. Much had to be done for him or he could not have accomplished all he did, but he gave far more than he took from others. How foolish it is for any of us to look at a twisted body, confined to a wheelchair, often in poor health, and say that such a life ought not to be permitted. His parents, and very many who knew him, were greatly enriched by this handicapped life. For him and for us it was a truly happy one. Let not mere man impugn either the wisdom or the goodness of God who gave him to us, and now has received him to the fuller life where no deficiencies can be known.'

Ray Ash was born fit and well, lived a physically vigorous life and seemed destined for missionary work until he was found to be suffering from the crippling disease of multiple sclerosis. His wife tells us more.

'Ray was at Bible College when symptoms of his illness first began to show themselves. He heard the results of his Bachelor of Divinity degree examination in hospital, the disease having already been diagnosed. He was told immediately of his probable, fairly rapid progress towards a wheelchair. He had multiple sclerosis, a progressively paralysing nervous disease which can rob a person of all movement and of every faculty before he dies from a side-effect of the actual disease.

'Ray was incredulous. He had come through strenuous war-time experiences, he had been fit and athletic, he was a missionary candidate waiting to go to the Far East with the Overseas Missionary Fellowship. How could it be that the Lord, for whom he wanted to do so much, should strike him down in this way rendering him seemingly useless for any form of service anywhere in the world? He could not believe that he had multiple sclerosis and went from doctor to doctor, convinced that the diagnosis would prove to be wrong, only to find that it really was true.

'How did he come through the period of turmoil, intense disappointment and frustration to the point of acceptance that his incurable disease was to be the means by which God would bring glory to Himself and through which He would use him as much, in a different way, as if he had become a missionary? He learned the lesson of acceptance in "the hard conflict of the soul". His pastor once asked Ray if he could discern anything of the purpose of God in his long years of increasing disability. His simple but profound answer was "that I might know God".

'As each year brought increased disability, until he had no use at all in his legs and very little in his arms, his testimony, spoken or unspoken, to the sustaining power of God reached and influenced more and more people. Euthanasia, had it been mentioned, would have been an unthinkable, abhorrent suggestion to him and to me. An illness to be accepted was the Lord's pathway for him and he would walk in it until the Lord called him to the place where there is no disability of body or mind.

'It was true that he had a great deal for which to be thankful. He was able to work for some years at the College where he had been a student, and until a few days before his death, with my help, he was still marking correspondence courses for the College. He had a home and a happy marriage. He was very much a part of the church of which he was a member, though he was seldom there in person. He made no concession to his illness and was much more concerned about the minor ailments of his friends than about his own incurable condition. Consequently he had many friends, including visitors from all over the world, and his life was full of interest.

'In retrospect it is easy to see the usefulness of his chronically disabled life. The radiance which shone from his face was like a benediction to those who visited him, even when he became too weak to speak much to them. But if, in the hopelessness and despair of the early years of the disease, when he suffered the indignity of having to submit to being in a wheelchair, of not being able to do one thing after another, some well-meaning person had suggested that his life was pointless and ought to be ended by himself, what a loss this would have been to very many people! His life was lived within very narrow physical confines, but it was lived to the full, and it was a privilege to be able to share it and to help to give his life this quality and fullness by just being, as it were, his arms and legs. Those who understood, knew that I gained at least as much as I gave.

'Ray died of pneumonia nearly twenty years after the onset of multiple sclerosis. It is a wonderful experience to watch a Christian die. The Lord gave Ray grace to endure the afflictions sent to him in life and He gave him grace to die, though in the extremity of weakness. We have a God, a heavenly Father, who is "too wise to err, too good to be unkind". He will give grace and glory and will bring His people home to Himself in His own time and way, which *must* be best for the one who dies and for those who are closely connected.'

While this book was being written I received the following letter:

'Having heard of your interest in the current euthanasia debate I thought you might like to hear of the experience I had of what some might call "passive euthanasia" when my father was dying last summer.

'When Dad went into hospital the surgeon had been very honest with him and explained that he expected to find a cancer, but that he hoped he would be able to remove it. At operation a tumour was found, but it was too advanced to remove and it had spread to the liver. Surgery could offer nothing and so the incision was closed.

'As I am a doctor I was asked whether I wanted my father to start drug therapy. This would not cure the cancer but would slow down its rate of growth. My experience of such treatment told me that it would be painful at worst and uncomfortable at best. Already Dad had indigestion and was not sleeping very well. There seemed little point in extending the duration of his symptoms. But for me, as a Christian, the most important fact was that God was in control and He had decided my father's life was to finish soon. It was not for me to decide to prolong it in these circumstances.

'My father had read in church to the congregation on the Sunday before going into hospital the twenty-third Psalm. "Even though I walk through the valley of the shadow of death I will fear no evil for Thou art with me. Thy rod and Thy staff comfort me."

'The decision to treat or not to treat was not a question of passive euthanasia, it was a question of bowing before the Almighty and saying, "Thy will be done."'

Further conversation with this correspondent revealed that his father had a significant influence in his village between the time of the operation and his death. For most people what he had to face would seem an appalling prospect. Yet his quiet confidence in God was that on leaving this life he would enter another which is better by far. For many it was the most vivid demonstration of the truth of the gospel that they had ever witnessed.

This is not an academic issue. These problems are real. They affect human beings like ourselves. They bring heartache and pain to husbands and wives, parents and children. We have not been discussing the disposal of obsolete machines or the emptying of dustbins. A sentence already quoted will bear repetition. 'The dilemma with which the doctor has to grapple is not an abstract problem in the field of ethical theory, but the practical question of what is proper treatment for an individual patient in particular circumstances.'[69]

So far, we have heard from those who have witnessed the life and death of people close to them. Before we turn from this issue let us hear what one who is still alive and well has to say.

'I was born twenty-eight years ago with spina bifida. There are people who say that babies born with this disablement, or any other like it, should not be allowed to live; that they should be put down at birth. Well, I have only got one thing to say to these people — they are talking rubbish. It is only animals that get put down, and we certainly are not animals. We are fully responsible human beings, although of course we do need a lot of help throughout our lives, and plenty of love too.

'I was given only a fortnight to live, two years at the most. I had a serious operation at eight days old on my spine. It was very close to my nervous system and the doctors did not think I would come through it. They said I would never use my hands. But I can write, sew etc. I can do practically anything with them. I never spoke until I was two and a half years old. Now I can say anything, even any big word. I am in a wheelchair but I am quite happy.

'I would like people who say that babies born disabled should be killed at birth to know that God put us on the earth like this for a purpose that only He knows; and when He wants us, He will take us. And if anyone else kills us at birth, they are going against the command that He gave us: "Thou shalt not kill." I am happy to know that I am in His care, as I am sure I have been all my life and as I will be for the rest of it.'[70]

We must accept that euthanasia attempts to

face real problems and that, by and large, its advocates are sincere and compassionate people. But that does not lead to an automatic acceptance of their solutions. Indeed, as we have seen, their case simply does not stand up to examination. Whether or not one takes a position which is based on the Bible, the case against euthanasia is very much stronger than the case for its introduction.

For euthanasia to receive the support of law would be disastrous, affecting society in general and family life in particular. It would make crime respectable and compassion despicable. Mutual trust between patient and doctor, the old and the young, handicapped and the fit, would be a thing of the past. The real benefits which suffering brings would largely be lost. The fight against terminal illness and handicapping disorders would yield to economic, not scientific, considerations. Our feeble, synthetic way of life would degenerate further into a pit of our own making where values are valueless, love is loveless and life is hopeless.

The case against euthanasia is so strong that it must win the day. Each of us must ensure that this is so. But the problems it was intended to solve will still be with us. What of those?

# 7.
# Help me to live and die

With each passing year the elderly mother grows older, more frail, less able to cope, and more burdened with anxiety about the future for her retarded son. The Aunty Marys of this world linger in the limbo between life and death, an apparently pointless existence which drains the state of funds and facilities which could otherwise help the young to live. In spite of the diligent research of concerned scientists, a cure for cancer still eludes them and in consequence the suffering continues until painful death.

Despair may make these people ask, 'Help me to die,' but their real longing is 'Help me to live.' How shall we do this? Are we merely to extend their painful or meaningless existence by adding empty days or years? That is no answer. These people need help to live and help to die. While breath is in them they must be nurtured and cared for and prepared in heart and mind for the day when death comes at God's time.

The question is 'How?'

## 1. Help me to live

Take the case of the retarded person for example.

When a handicapped baby is born the parents and their medical advisors should adopt a realistic, but positive attitude to this new young life. No one can predict with certainty how retarded the child will be, how much or how little progress it may make, how much support it will require, or how fulfilled its life might become. But if, from its earliest days, all involved determine to maximize its potential it will certainly make far greater progress than if it is left to unimaginative and unstimulating care.

However, the parents will need help, and not only from the professional bodies and services. Encouragement and support must be forthcoming from the community, too — from us. Fear of mentally handicapped children often results in parents feeling isolated. They have difficulty with shopping, and rarely have an evening out as no one will baby-sit for them. They suffer the unfeeling disinterest of others or, worse, their hostility.

Churches have not shown themselves too willing to help either. Mentally handicapped people are not readily welcomed in Sunday Schools or services. Christian involvement in societies for the retarded is rare. There is room for a greater measure of concern at this point, and of practical support.

Then consider what happens when the retarded child becomes a retarded adult. There is very little hope at the moment of his being provided with a caring home in the community once his parents can no longer cope with this responsibility. The facts speak for themselves. There is need for about 60,000 such places in hostels in England and Wales. When Mum dies the authorities will have to make room for yet another bed in a hospital for the subnormal, and the rest of his days will be spent in crowded conditions which do not meet his real needs.

The documentary *Silent Minority* (1981) exposed horrifyingly low levels of staffing in some wards of subnormality hospitals. The 'care' filmed by camera men would be described as 'neglect' if it took place outside of a hospital. Stories circulate from time to time of brutal treatment of patients in such places. What sort of prospect is that for a parent, or a retarded person, to have to face?

If only there were some other alternative, some Christian alternative. Is it beyond the wit of God's people to set up homes for such as these retarded adults? The cost is immense and the responsibility long term, but cash and know-how are not the greatest problems. With faith and persistence both can be overcome. The real issue is whether Christians care enough to do it. Already a start is being made by Christian Concern for the Mentally Handicapped, among others. There is opportunity for many more to be involved and for much more to be done.

Many elderly people will eventually find themselves in need of the care and shelter which others must provide for them, but if Christians care they need not be abandoned to geriatric wards and left to rot. The greatest single factor leading to the decay of mind is the feeling that one is unwanted, that one is not needed, that there is no longer any purpose in living. If we practise what we profess, then no one belonging to our church — and perhaps a wider circle too — must be allowed to feel like that.

Every part of the body of Christ is important to the whole. This is true of the local church as of the whole church. It is as true of the elderly as of the young, of the retarded, as of the intellectual. Therefore there should be a concern for and interest in every Christian within our particular fellowship. The stimulus of interested and interesting friends can keep old people lively in mind long after their bodies have slowed to a snail's pace. They need to be visited, encouraged, talked to and (perhaps most important), listened to by those who are still active.

If the time comes when their powers fail and they are no longer able to live at home, Christians could provide the homes they will need in their frail old age. Some are already doing this. There are Christian societies trying to meet part of this great need. Some churches have set up their own home for the elderly on spare land on their site or elsewhere. Such schemes deserve the encouragement and support of every Christian, but there is still the need to maintain the loving interest of friends or fellow-members when Aunty Mary moves into care of this sort.

Alternatively, it may be possible for her to stay at home, given the right sort of professional and personal support. Sister Harriet Copperman provides home care for dying patients and their families in a London borough. She made some telling observations in the magazine of Age Concern.

'"Home is where the heart is" and as we grow older the heart tends to settle more and more on the familiar and comfortable surroundings of a home which has taken shape over the years. How difficult then to leave such a place at a time of life when it is most needed — when illness and death are approaching. It is hard to be transported in a bumpy ambulance to a strange hospital bed, knowing that you will never see home again, never see the tomatoes ripen again, as they have year after year. Never again have the dog sitting at the end of the bed. Never again have a cup of tea made by the wife who has made it for the last forty years, and never again share a warm and comforting bed with her.

'In recent years there has been a tendency to put people into hospital when the end of life approaches... There is also a tendency to believe that the best care available is in a hospital or similar setting because "they can do such marvellous things these days"...

'However, this trend towards dying in hospital may be reversible. More thought and care is being given to the ageing and dying. At the same time, with shrinking financial resources, it is becoming apparent to the authorities that it is cheaper to care for someone in his own home than in hospital, and in any event, bed closures are making it increasingly difficult to admit dying patients into hospital.'[71]

Perhaps a new opportunity is opening up for us to show that Christians really do care.

Of course these suggestions will cost money. But with wages higher than ever, there should be more money available for such projects — if only we could keep our own standard of living in check.

And the suggestions will also cost time. Again, we have more leisure hours than ever our predecessors had, and the help of labour-saving devices. Surely some of that time can be rescued for the ministry of caring which is our responsibility. And with so many Christians faced with unemployment, surely a part of their time and their energies could be devoted to this sort of caring activity.

There is one other group to mention, and it is the most difficult of all. What of those who are dying in agony? They may be only a small proportion of those who are sick and dying but the fact that they are suffering makes them significant. We cannot turn unfeelingly away from them. Yet it is just here we may seem most helpless for surely there is little we can do to help.

'We are now always able to control pain in terminal cancer in the patient sent to us, and only very rarely do we have to make them continually asleep in so doing.'[72]

Dr Cicely Saunders wrote these words as long ago as 1961, and there have been many advances since then. From her Hospice in South London Dr Saunders has shown the way to care for the dying and their families. Her experience is matched by that of Dr Robert G. Twycross, Medical Director of a Hospice in the grounds of Churchill Hospital, Oxford.

'Together with Doctor Saunders and other experts in the field, Doctor Twycross has made the extensive studies which now allow very severe pain to be controlled to a remarkable degree, while maintaining alertness of patients in modern hospices. By means of polypharmacy — the use of many different medications in a single situation — he adjusts each patient's regimen, and readjusts it as often as necessary to keep the individual comfortable and in a normal frame of mind while out-manoeuvring the central nervous system's messages of agony. Bone pain, for example, which is apt to be particularly savage and intractable, is managed under the system with the aid of powerful anti-inflammatory drugs, as well as the usual Hospice Mix containing diamorphine as its basic ingredient. The "double nature" of pain is carefully monitored, met not only with proper analgesics and tender care for the individual, but with an honest relationship which the patient can trust.'[73]

Hospices are also springing up all over America with an additional dimension yet to be developed in Britain. 'Hospice teams' have been formed in many districts made up of volunteers who are willing to share in the care of the dying in their own homes. Some are professionals — nurses, doctors, social workers etc. Some are just concerned to give help, to run errands, to sit with the sick person, and to assist in any way possible. Thus they provide medical, nursing and compassionate care for people in their own homes and among their own families. In due course institutions may become an essential part of such schemes, but in this way a start has been made to care for those whose need is *now*.

Once again, this is an area of need where Christian doctors, nurses and church members can become involved and make a significant contribution to the pressing needs around them. This, too, will make considerable demands in terms of time and money. But above all, it will demand our love — or rather, recourse to God's love through us.

Some Christians will find these suggestions difficult. While they will agree in opposing euthanasia they will draw back from the alternative solutions proposed. In their view the sort of social involvement envisaged is secondary — even if permissible. They may belong to a brand of evangelicalism unique to our own century, which not only draws a sharp distinction between evangelism and social concern, it builds a wall between the two, and tops it with barbed wire.

Scripture is rich in direct commands, clear examples and plain instructions about our duty towards those in need. It urges us to recognize our responsibility towards one another as human beings. The implied answer to Cain's question: 'Am I my brother's keeper?' is a resounding 'Yes, you are'. It is unthinkable that we should be so isolated from other people that we can excuse indifference to their needs.

That responsibility is not merely a matter of our common humanity. It is also a matter of law — God's law. We are commanded to love our neighbour as ourselves. Throughout the Bible it is plain that our 'neighbour' is a person in need rather than someone who happens to live next door. Israel was soundly told off by God's prophets on several occasions even though they were carefully maintaining their religious rituals. It was because of their lack of care for the poor and needy which God regarded as flagrant disobedience. Today that law still stands — for Christian and non-Christian.

The strongest motivation for the Christian, however, is not law but love. If God's love has been 'poured out into our hearts' then it must show itself in real life. It will not be surprising if its demonstration parallels the behaviour of Jesus. He 'went about doing good' — healing, helping, encouraging, supporting. Can you imagine the Saviour walking through a cancer ward with his eyes on the ceiling, only willing to pause if someone expressed 'spiritual' interest?

There is no escaping the fact that God intends Christians, in particular, to engage in a practical 'ministry' of compassion. See how He has stated it plainly. 'For it is by grace you have been saved, through faith — and this not from yourselves, it is the gift of God — not by works, so that no one can boast, for we are God's workmanship, created in Christ Jesus to do good works, which God prepared in advance for us to do.'[74]

## 2. Help me to die

There is one more thing to say. Even when we have helped people to live, the time will come when we must also help them to die. We have no interest in extending life by a few more days, weeks or years simply for the sake of doing so. We must help people to live with dignity and to die with dignity. And no philosophy or religion is better equipped to do both than that which we find in the Bible. We have already considered the distinctiveness of human beings in the world, and that extends also to their death. We believe that death is not like putting out a candle, with nothing more than a smoke of memories lingering on the air for a short time, and then oblivion. There is something beyond it, and we must be prepared before the final hour strikes for us.

The gospel of the Lord Jesus Christ, and that only, can make a person so ready for death that not only is its approach not terrifying, but it may even positively be welcomed. Beyond the seeming blackness of death is the prospect of meeting the most wonderful Person who has ever lived, and of spending an unending eternity in the direct enjoyment of His company. And we understand from the Bible that the pleasures of a perfect heaven are such that we cannot begin to understand how desirable they are.[75]

That may seem very well in theory, but what of the practical outworking of it? When a person's life is ebbing away how can they be helped to face the approach of death, and the nearness of eternity? Whether it be warning or encouragement that must be given, somehow fear must be neutralized and replaced by hope.

*a. A new attitude*
The first problem to be faced is one of attitude: the attitude of both the dying person and those who would help him. Both must learn a right attitude to death. That which prevails in society today is almost entirely negative. It avoids mention of the subject, discourages attendance at funerals, or − as in America − so embellishes death as to make it seem unreal, even alive.

This attitude of rejection might claim biblical support, for death is called 'the last enemy'. Of course, there is a sense in which it is alien to us. It is part of the curse we bear from the rebellion of Eden's garden. It seems to rob us of our most precious possession − life itself. It comes between the choicest relationships, severs the deepest ties.

Then, too, death is apparently so final and so unknown. Anyone who has been suddenly bereft of a loved father or wife or son, knows how long it takes to realize that that person really has gone from one's life. The footstep on the stair, the key in the lock, the telephone call might all be theirs, but are not. The curtain has fallen never to rise again; the door has closed never to open once more. So far as this world and this life is concerned death is really *the end*.

Yet we feel deeply that it cannot be all. Brave atheists have written stirring lines about facing their end, but many have paused at its brink to ponder. Can all the ingenuity, wisdom and spiritual force disappear like smoke on the breeze when a man dies? Everything in us feels there must be more. We are not mere animals, or shadows. But who can know what follows those dread moments when the heart stops its beating and the brain its thinking? Will there be a conscious existence, perhaps a shadowy world through which to roam, never finding or arriving, or journeys to be taken in vessels thoughtfully provided by loved ones, or heaven, or hell?

All of us, healthy or dying, must learn that death is a part of living. It is 'the experience of a lifetime' through which we shall all pass and do well to face now. Though it will end, at least for a time, all our earthly relationships, some relationships can survive its dreadful stroke. Much of what will follow death cannot be known, but some of its mysteries can be understood here and now for God has given us much needed information.

If death is a part of life then dying is a part of living. It has been said that we need time to die. We need time to adjust to new perspectives and priorities. A young doctor dying from cancer wrote of it in this way: 'Dying makes life suddenly real. Watching my slow physical deterioration reaffirmed my belief that there is something else within, which would survive if only because my personality stayed the same in spite of the eroding bodily form in which it is confined. Slowly I have come to terms with my own circumstances, though each must find his own way to resolve the conflict.'[76]

If we are to help people to die we must adopt those changed perspectives for ourselves, at least while we are with them. We shall want to keep their interest in family and friends warm and vital, but we do them no service by talking endless trivialities. They and we must be able openly to discuss what faces them. So far as what remains of this life is concerned, we must ease their passage as much as we can by thoughtful, caring encouragement to the dying person. 'Terminal illness should not be regarded as an intrusion into life; it is part of life and can be a time of increasing maturity and deepening spiritual experience for all concerned.'[77]

If this new attitude to death is adopted it will help both the dying person and those about him. We who live can be of real help to the person who needs meaningful support at the approach of the ultimate experience of death.

'Death is probably the loneliest experience any of us will ever have to face. Those who are dying reach out for support and companionship to trusted advisors and to those they love most. If the doctor "fobs" off his patient's questions with glib and false answers the patient will soon realize that the doctor does not consider him capable of being told the truth. He then turns to his wife, whose anxiety is obvious, only to be told that "everything is coming along nicely. The doctor said you will be up in no time." The patient knows this is untrue and, after a few such experiences, feels totally alone, retreats more and more into himself and becomes increasingly dejected and lonely. On the other hand, the emotional isolation of the dying may be diminished if all who care for him are aware of the problem and treat the patient with kindness, understanding and as an intelligent adult capable of adjusting to the truth. The forced kiss of a visiting relative, the artificial jocularity of a workmate tell the suspicious patient all he needs to know about his prognosis. The helpless feeling of the sick man can be seen in his expression which implies, "You wouldn't tell me the truth, even if I asked you."

'Communication is not just a matter of words. Holding a patient's hand while talking to him, even an arm round his shoulder conveys a positive message, "No matter what happens I shall stand by you — I won't let you down." Similarly, sitting on the bed or on a chair beside the bed means that the doctor is not going to keep his distance, but is prepared to meet the patient on the patient's own terms.'[78]

Then, too, it will affect the attitude of the dying person to what is happening to him. It must do so. To quote again from the young doctor writing of the approach of his own death: 'Strange to relate, however, my life as a practising Christian was changed by the knowledge that I was dying almost more than if I had been a committed atheist. Suddenly all I had been told or read in the Bible made sense. My life-style didn't change very much but my attitude did; it was as if I suddenly started really to live, although the reverse was true and I was dying. A clear spring morning is most meaningful after weeks of dull wet weather. The slow build-up of dust on a car windscreen goes unnoticed until I clean it with a few squirts of water and the windscreen wipers. So life can really be understood when it is contrasted with death.

'This is impossible for a normal healthy person to accept, it just doesn't make sense . . . Once the celestial city comes into view — to use the analogy from Bunyan's story — life is never quite the same. For me I suddenly became free, free to live as a person in my own right.'[79] Which brings us to another important aspect of helping the dying.

*b. A new hope*
John Bunyan captures the contrasting experiences some face as they stand on the brink of death. In *Pilgrim's Progress* Hopeful waded into the river boldly and clear-eyed, urged on by the sight of the Celestial City beyond. Meanwhile Christian trembled and stumbled fearfully into that awful stream. The memory of past sins and the troubling of evil spirits obscured his confidence in God's promises. But his friend Hopeful continued to support and encourage him until he found ground beneath his feet and followed it to the far side of the river. For both of them the prospect was identical, while in one hope rose with greater strength.

So there is hope. But not for **selfish enjoyment**. The Christian has a duty to **make that hope** public knowledge. He is not to keep it to himself, as if he belonged to a secret society. It is to be publicized as widely as possible so that the greatest possible number of people are released from their terror of death, and given this hope. Or to put it in more traditional terms — the Christian is to evangelize so that people will be saved from condemnation and despair, and find life in Christ.

Evangelism has a direct bearing on our subject. We must help people to die. When a sick man is nearing his end he often has a premonition of the fact. His family may try to hide it from him with the doctor's collusion. They may be afraid that he cannot face the inevitable, that it is therefore better for him not to know. Or they may simply be afraid to put into words what they know about his condition. Someone needs to tell him, kindly and, more than that, to help him face what that means both for him and for his family. He can then begin to adjust his sights, as it were. He may well begin to think of 'the hereafter'. And he may want to know how, at so late a stage, Christ can give him hope as He did to one of the two thieves who were crucified with Him. And, like that thief, the dying man may be helped to die with the dignity of knowing that he is a child of God.

There is another way in which evangelism is relevant. If we win the people of our generation to Christ it will make for a more humane society. They will then more readily accept that we do not have the right or the authority to decide on the lives and deaths of others. It should also make for a more compassionate society, too, if more people are motivated by the love of God. More money will be available for those in need. More time can be given to help them. More can then be accomplished and, of course, more people will be freed from their terror of death. More will share in the hope of which the Bible speaks, and thus be made happy.

If we are silent, who will speak? If we are careless, who will care? Shall we, Pilate-like, try to wash our hands when death-dealing legislation is passed in our land? But who are *you* to protest? Who will take any notice? I reply, you are a citizen with a vote. You have a Member of Parliament, a local or county councillor to represent you at national and local level. You can and should let them know your views on these things. You have access to local papers and local radio, with as much right for your views to be publicized as those who advocate euthanasia. You have friends whom you may influence by talking to them. You have fellow Christians whom you may arouse by discussions. And you are surrounded by people for whom you may and must care.

'People are special and human life is sacred, whether we admit it or not. Every life is precious and worthwhile in itself — not only to us human beings but also to God. Every person is worth fighting for, regardless of whether he is young or old, sick or well, child or adult, born or unborn, or brown, red, yellow, black or white.'[80]

# References

1. Dame Eileen Younghusband, 'The Right to Die', *Community Care,* 29.3.78, p.16.
2. *ibid.,* p.16.
3. G. C. Scorer, *Life in our Hands,* Inter-Varsity Press, p.132.
4. *ibid.,* p.132.
5. Marya Mannes, *Last Rights,* Millington, p.127.
6. Quotations from EXIT in this chapter are taken from the publicity material of EXIT and their booklet *The Last Right.*
7. Dr E. Koop and Dr F. Schaeffer, *Whatever Happened to the Human Race?,* Marshall, Morgan & Scott, p.77.
8. Scorer, *op. cit.,* p.135.
9. Mannes, *op. cit.,* p.31.
10. As no.6.
11. T. Beauchamp & S. Perkin (Ed), *Ethical Issues in Death and Dying,* Prentice, Hall Inc., p.217.
12. Koop & Schaeffer, *op. cit.,* p.79.
13. Quoted by Koop & Schaeffer, *op. cit.,* p.76.
14. Younghusband, *op. cit.*
15. Mannes, *op. cit.,* p.77.
16. Younghusband, *op. cit.*
17. Glanville Williams in Beauchamp & Perkin, *op. cit.,* p.232.
18. Mannes, *op. cit.,* p.63.
19. Quoted by William Purcell in *New Age,* Volume 12, Autumn 1980.
20. As no.6.
21. Glanville Williams, *op. cit.,* p.239.
22. Koop & Schaeffer, *op. cit.,* p.76.
23. Quoted in Koop & Schaeffer, *op. cit.,* p.76.
24. Younghusband, *op. cit.*
25. *Daily Express,* 4.12.79.
26. *EXIT Newsletter,* Spring 1980.
27. Romans 14:7.
28. Dr Frohman quoted by Y. Kamisar in Beauchamp & Perkins, *op. cit.,* p.222.
29. *ibid.,* p.222.
30. D. Vere, *Voluntary Euthanasia,* CMF, p.18.
31. Dr A. Clark, 'Death on Demand', *New Age,* Vol.12, Autumn 1980.

32. Sharpe in *Medication as a Threat to Testamentary Capacity*, quoted by Y. Kamisar, *op. cit.*, p.222.
33. B. Miller quoted by Y. Kamisar, *ibid.*, p.222.
34. House of Lords Debate 103, Vth Series, 1936, Col.466.
35. D. Vere, *op. cit.*, p.41.
36. Dr A. L. Wolbarst quoted by Y. Kamisar, *op. cit.*, p.225.
37. Dr B. Miller quoted by Y. Kamisar, *ibid.*, p.226.
38. D. Vere, *op. cit.*, p.13.
39. J. Rostan quoted in *The Right to Live, the Right to Die*, Dr E. Koop, Tyndale House Publishers, flyleaf.
40. Job 12:10.
41. Psalm 31:15.
42. Acts 17:28.
43. Ecclesiastes 3:2.
44. Ecclesiastes 8:7,8 (NIV margin).
45. Genesis 9:6.
46. Exodus 20:13.
47. Koop & Schaeffer, *op. cit.*, p.88.
48. Jeremiah 1:5.
49. Acts 9:15.
50. Acts 2:23.
51. H. M. Carson, *Facing Suffering*, Evangelical Press, pp.53-54.
52. J. Wenham, *The Goodness of God*, Inter-Varsity Press, pp.83-84.
53. Dr R. G. Twycross, *The Dying Patient*, CMF, p.5.
54. Twycross, *ibid.*, p.16.
55. Sandol Stoddard, *The Hospice Movement*, Jonathan Cape, pp.2-4.
56. Sir Norman Anderson, *Issues of Life & Death*, Hodder & Stoughton, pp.100-101.
57. *ibid.*, pp.108-109.
58. Koop, *op. cit.*, pp.98-99.
59. Anderson, *op. cit.*, pp.101-102.
60. *The Times*, 6.11.81.
61. *ibid.*
62. Exodus 4:11.
63. Dr G. Wenham, *Third Way*, August 1981.
64. *ibid.*
65. *The Times*, 6.11.81.
66. Quoted in *The Guardian*, 28.10.81.
67. *The Sunday Times*, 8.11.81.
68. as 59.
69. *ibid.*, p.102.
70. Lyn Jones, *Evangelical Times*, June 1981, p.9.
71. Sister H. Copperman, *New Age*, Vol.12, Autumn 1980, p.12.
72. Dr C. Saunders, *Lancet*, 2.9.61.
73. Stoddard, *op. cit.*, p.183.
74. Ephesians 2:8-10.
75. 1 Corinthians 2:9,10.

76. Dr James Casson, *Dying, the Greatest Adventure of my Life*, CMF, p.6.
77. Twycross, *op. cit.*, p.21.
78. *ibid.*, pp.7-8.
79. Casson, *op. cit.*, p.19.
80. Koop & Schaeffer, *op. cit.*, p.156.